T0365712

Cambridge Elements

Elements in Critical Heritage Studies
edited by
Kristian Kristiansen
University of Gothenburg
Michael Rowlands
UCL

THE NEOLIBERALISATION OF HERITAGE IN AFRICA

Rachel King
*University College London and University
of the Witwatersrand*

CAMBRIDGE
UNIVERSITY PRESS

Shaftesbury Road, Cambridge CB2 8EA, United Kingdom

One Liberty Plaza, 20th Floor, New York, NY 10006, USA

477 Williamstown Road, Port Melbourne, VIC 3207, Australia

314–321, 3rd Floor, Plot 3, Splendor Forum, Jasola District Centre, New Delhi – 110025, India

103 Penang Road, #05–06/07, Visioncrest Commercial, Singapore 238467

Cambridge University Press is part of Cambridge University Press & Assessment, a department of the University of Cambridge.

We share the University's mission to contribute to society through the pursuit of education, learning and research at the highest international levels of excellence.

www.cambridge.org
Information on this title: www.cambridge.org/9781009548250

DOI: 10.1017/9781009435321

© Rachel King 2025

This publication is in copyright. Subject to statutory exception and to the provisions of relevant collective licensing agreements, no reproduction of any part may take place without the written permission of Cambridge University Press & Assessment.

When citing this work, please include a reference to the DOI 10.1017/9781009435321

First published 2025

A catalogue record for this publication is available from the British Library

ISBN 978-1-009-54825-0 Hardback
ISBN 978-1-009-43529-1 Paperback
ISSN 2632-7074 (online)
ISSN 2632-7066 (print)

Cambridge University Press & Assessment has no responsibility for the persistence or accuracy of URLs for external or third-party internet websites referred to in this publication and does not guarantee that any content on such websites is, or will remain, accurate or appropriate.

The Neoliberalisation of Heritage in Africa

Elements in Critical Heritage Studies

DOI: 10.1017/9781009435321
First published online: January 2025

Rachel King
University College London and University of the Witwatersrand
Author for correspondence: Rachel King, rachel-king@ucl.ac.uk

Abstract: The landscape of heritage on the African continent is the product of neoliberal economic and social interventions from the 1980s to the 2000s: the prevalence and influence of heritage NGOs; aid for cultural programmes contingent on government reforms; the use of national heritage policies and projects to signal ready capital; experiments in custodianship and private enterprise that balance conservation with consumerism; and so on. This Element synthesises literature from anthropology, archaeology, history, and geography to describe a significant period of heritage policy and discourse on the African continent – its historical situation, on-the-ground realities, and continuing legacies in the era of sustainable development and climate crises.

Keywords: heritage, development, Africa, neoliberalism, structural adjustment

ISBNs: 9781009548250 (HB), 9781009435291 (PB), 9781009435321 (OC)
ISSNs: 2632-7074 (online), 2632-7066 (print)

Contents

1 The Heritage of Neoliberal Development

The period from roughly the 1980s to the 2010s witnessed the increasing entanglement of heritage and neoliberal development. We can see this in the proliferation of terms that we now take for granted within heritage studies: stakeholders, stewards, governance, capacity building, grassroots, and so on. A small, but significant, corpus of anthropological research has demonstrated the importance of examining how the value of the past is shaped by economic interests and promoted by transnational, national, and sub-national actors (e.g. Meskell 2012; Lafrenz Samuels 2018; Luke 2019; De Cesari 2020; Labadi 2022). This literature leads onto the questions underpinning this Element: How do neoliberal ways of being and acting affect practices of care and knowledge-making associated with heritage? What can we learn by treating neoliberalism as an intellectual instrument that has shaped practices of caring for and making heritage? And what are the consequences of these processes for heritage studies as a field? This latter, more reflexive question is significant because – as we will see shortly – the process of leveraging heritage for development has not automatically produced greater attention to actual substance of the past itself.

This Element is thus about a historical moment as well as a way of thinking about sovereignty, aspiration, consumption, and morality in novel ways that are only available through heritage. It advances new, multidimensional understandings of how heritage has been shaped by the policy interventions, financial webs, visions, and critiques that have come to sit under the heading of neoliberalism in Africa. These themes have previously been dispersed across disciplinary literatures and are synthesised here for the first time.

This is not to suggest, however, that there is a consensus on the definition of neoliberalism. The opposite is true, particularly as the proliferation of scholarship in and about development, heritage, and Africa is not always accompanied by a rigorous unpacking of the epistemologies at work across the disciplines involved (Rico and King 2024). At its broadest, neoliberalism encompasses principles of governance and economics: neoliberalism favours market growth and private responsibility for welfare, health, and other social values; it rejects government as the central or primary institution of social protection and economic regulation (Craig and Porter 2006: 5–7; Brown 2015). In Africa, neoliberal doctrine is closely associated with the structural adjustment programmes (SAPs) of the 1980s and 1990s, implemented by the International Monetary Fund (IMF) and the World Bank (also referred to here as 'the Bank') as a means of reducing government waste and helping 'Global South' economies to function more effectively (Ndulu 2008; Harrison 2019; Decker and McMahon 2020: 160–163). Neoliberal reforms on the continent are also evident where they have widened inequalities, fuelled scepticism in the state's ability to provide for its citizens, and imbued markets (rather than governments) with the power to determine how to value public resources (Hart 2002; James 2014; Wiegratz 2016; Fredericks 2018). Thirty years on, the effects of these interventions are entrenched and pervasive, and have amounted to nothing short of moral and ethical engineering (Wiegratz 2016). The history of these reforms means that '"neoliberalism" in Africa refers to a quite fundamentally different situation than it does in Western Europe and North America', and shores up images of Africa as under- or un-developed (Ferguson 1994: xiii–xiv, 2010: 173).

However, we can also refuse a monolithic conception of neoliberalism. This is supported by global treatments of neoliberalism as a political and practical field, derived from economic doctrine but ultimately diverted from this by particular actors and policy programmes (Harvey 2005). We can approach these through an analytic considering both 'the nature of the agencies that drive neoliberal reform, and the extent to which neoliberal reform agendas impact upon broader social relations' (Harrison 2005: 1306). These experiences are fundamentally social, occurring within multiple overlapping spatial and scalar arenas – and therefore available for anthropological and historical examination (Wiegratz et al. 2022).

Consequently, the functions and fault lines of neoliberalism have been examined through so many phenomena on the African continent – higher education (Mbembe 2016), infrastructure (Chalfin 2001; Larkin 2008), nature conservation (Brockington 2002) – that we may well ask why heritage has come off relatively lightly (but see Meskell 2012). These and other previous discussions have highlighted the tendency for neoliberalism to become a floating signifier, easily unmoored from intellectual, geographical, and institutional contexts and attached to things that conventional wisdom has dictated are broadly to do with the global free market (Ferguson 2010; Fredericks 2018). Further, a central problem of locating heritage within development thinking and planning is that it is rarely mentioned by name: culture and heritage are not equivalent but have been used interchangeably in the language of development (Cross and Giblin 2023), leaving scholars to discern a role for heritage from multiple successive development frameworks. There is thus an imperative to bring heritage into the nuanced analytical view afforded by decades of scholarship from cognate fields.

This Element therefore advances two arguments, which demonstrate how African experiences hold planetary significance for heritage studies (Coombe and Weiss 2015; Meskell 2021). First, the fingerprints of neoliberal interventions are evident – although under-appreciated – in the practice of heritage on the African continent, and in the institutions and collectives who shape and are shaped by it. The unified field of vision articulated here for the first time allows us to appreciate the full scope of these legacies: the industries, products, and authorities that have come to constitute the field of heritage but are too often seen disparately in disciplines dominated by case studies and partitioned by methodology (Rico and King 2024). Examining how heritage value is made within the neoliberalising dynamics of African countries demonstrates the extent to which this is subject to the same forces of governance and market intervention that affected other areas of life (compare Hart 2002: 12–13 with Coombe and Weiss 2015): from agricultural science in Sudan (see below) to cattle vaccinations in Tanzania (Section 3) and road-building in Mauritania (Section 4). Through this approach we can understand how heritage has helped shape territorial sovereignty, even while this is being undermined in other areas of governance (Section 2); follow heritage entrepreneurs to resolve contradictions between communalist and individualist claims to benefit from the past (Section 3); and trace connections from development funding to knowledge about the past (Section 4).

Second, I show that the work of neoliberalism is far from finished and, like all successful global paradigms, it has become embedded in the things and processes that we take for granted. We need to unpick these to see how they function, not least because neoliberalism deliberately obscures its historical roots. Development activities, methodologies, agents, and agencies on the African continent have roots in extractivist and missionising notions of social improvement, meaning that development is itself a form of heritage with a long reach. Consequently, we can look to views of those long-term betterment programmes to understand how the past has been leveraged in the service of progress and paternalism; of selective remembering and forgetting when progress fails to deliver; and of resilience when development-affected people utilise intergenerational experiences to navigate more recent efforts at 'upliftment'. This Element is necessary to demonstrate that many of the things we have taken as the truisms of heritage as aligned to development – its forward-looking orientation, its transnational and multicultural values – are *derived from* neoliberal thinking.

1.1 Development without a Past: Ahistoricism and Adjustment

Perhaps the most specific place to begin a heritage-focused exploration of neoliberalism is as a form of intentional development that promotes a generally ahistorical view of the past. The rise of neoliberal development is a well-rehearsed narrative. Following World War II, development became increasingly internationalised as multilateral agencies like the United Nations (UN), its subsidiaries, and international financial institutions (IFIs) succeeded imperial powers in facilitating the modernisation of under-developed countries. Development theory in the 1950s–1970s was broadly based on long-term (historical) and comparative analysis of socio-economic changes in 'traditional' and industrialised countries (Hart 2001: 651). Particularly for African countries during the 1960s (when many were gaining independence), there was an emphasis on reforms like rapid industrialisation and mass consumption aimed at producing self-sustaining states (Decker and McMahon 2020: 156). By the 1980s, the economic policies of the world's major financial institutions coalesced around the position that inefficient government and over-regulation of domestic markets were preventing nations in the under-developed 'Global South' (which included almost all of Africa) from prospering. The solution (exemplified in the Washington Consensus) was that governments should privatise and deregulate domestic markets, reduce fiscal deficits, and open trade and capital accounts to a global free market (Williamson 1993), which amounted to assessing modernisation through a focus on economic performance (Hart 2001: 651).

This transition was galvanised by the implementation of SAPs and ultimately constituted a paradigm shift within development thinking: from historicism to ahistoricism and a particular kind of nationalism. This happened at a methodological level at the Bank and the IMF (among others), where the gross domestic product (GDP) growth rate, the balance of fiscal and external payments, and the rate of inflation were key metrics for assessing how efficiently economies allocated resources. Not only did domestic policies and national factors become key to explaining these criteria, but 'the dynamics of long-term transformations of economies and societies slipped from view' (Gore 2000: 794–795). The rapid growth of a corps of American scientific consultants, contingent on an expanded educational system and training oriented towards short-term intervention over long-term investment, also helped to institutionalise ahistoricism in international development (Decker and McMahon 2020: 156–157). That said, the transition to independence in many African states saw colonial experts move into roles at UN agencies or remain in-country as consultants within re-invented or new bureaucratic structures. The dawn of the 'development era' thus featured reconfigured, but still familiar, colonial personnel and institutions (Frey and Kunkel 2011: 223). This tension between continuity and short-termism is, I argue, part of what a view of development as heritage can highlight and I return to it next.

The SAPs propagated under an orthodox neoliberal model of development became a hallmark of African experiences of the 1980s and 1990s: receiving international financing was contingent on scaling back the role of the regulatory state and its spending in favour of privatisation, with the result that devolved and non-state entities (especially civil society and non-governmental organisations [NGOs]) increasingly took on the job of governing, while national industries and infrastructures became increasingly available for private investment (Ferguson 2006). The consequences of the SAPs were not, however, more effective governance and economic growth but rather their opposites. Economists of and from the continent as well as African heads of state had warned as much, while also asserting capacity for development within the continent via multilateral declarations like the 1979 Monrovia Declaration, the 1980 Lagos Plan of Action, and the 1985 Final Act of Lagos (Mkandawire and Soludo 2003: 2–4).

When the failures of SAPs became apparent there ensued a pivot from a strict focus on the classic metrics of performance towards a perspective expansive enough to consider sociocultural conditions. The Bank cited (especially sub-Saharan) Africa as evidence of a need for a new, gentler approach to development that invested in (among other 'fundamentals') human resources and regional co-operation (Mkandawire and Soludo 2003: 5–6). This shift led to the emphasis on participation, civil society, and culture that has come to characterise neoliberal development in its more humane alignment with participatory development (Watts 2006). These and later revisionist attempts did not so much scrap the key tenets of neoliberal doctrine as fracture them in such a way that they persist in successive modes of thinking about and implementing socio-economic progress: the ongoing limited role of the state in public life; promoting increasingly globalised marketplaces; re-defining the reach and role of 'the local'; among others. Moreover, the move towards participatory development did not inherently entail a greater attention to historical context, as we shall see.

1.2 African Knowledge for African Development

Well before the heyday of SAPs academics writing from the African continent had called for a greater historicism in charting development priorities, with a particular focus on identifying resources for development from within Africa. Walter Rodney's (2012: 62) description of 'underdevelopment' is among the most influential references for this contrast, notable for his objection to seeking African modes of development in 'comparisons with European "civilizations"'. This was not the first attempt to historicise poverty on the continent (e.g. Marxist and substantivist anthropological approaches of the 1950s and 1960s), and explanations related to the particularities of African situations (the availability of land and labour, the nature of state formation, the transatlantic slave trade) expanded the perspectives on socio-economic history available from the 1970s (Akyeampong et al. 2014: 2–4).

At the height of adjustment programmes and in their long aftermath scholars
of African history and culture issued clear rebukes to development agencies and
actors for their ahistoricism and cultural ignorance. In his address to the 2001
African Studies Association, Eisha Odhiambo (2002: 2) took the opportunity to
reflect on the inadequacies of the Bank's engagement with African culture and
its past:

> To put it bluntly, with the failure of the Structural Adjustment Programmes to
> actually improve living standards in the decade and a half that they were in
> place, neoliberalism needed to find a reason for their failure outside the
> policies themselves. Hence the reemergence of the discourse on culture as
> a barrier to development.

Odhiambo's critique locates the relationship between culture and development
within a longer, broader conversation among African intellectuals about whether
one can productively consider a distinctly African 'personality' and worldview,
and if so how this can contribute to African development. These vibrant debates
saw pre-eminent scholars like Bethwell Ogot (1999) arguing for cultural heritage
as key to a more participatory process of mobilising Indigenous knowledge;
Paulin Hountondji (1995: 6–8) suggesting that 'age-old heritage' could be 'critically reappropriated' to overcome the 'dependence machine' of development;
and Valentin Mudimbe (1988: x) urging that reappropriation along these lines
should beware of reaffirming ultimately Eurocentric 'categories and conceptual
systems'. Nevertheless, these ideas remained marginal to or absent from development thinking that stubbornly viewed 'custom and tradition' as 'some kind of
heavy burden that Africa must carry' (Odhiambo 2002: 11).

1.3 'Culture' for Development Is Not Equivalent to 'Pasts' for Development

The 'cultural turn' within development that accompanied the softening of
adjustment would eventually create a space for recognising what these scholars
had long insisted,[1] but only after neoliberal orthodoxy had wrought significant
effects on the continent. At the same time, a strain of thought in development
thinking that viewed culture as likely to *impede* social cohesion (and therefore
progress) remained pervasive (Labadi 2018: 44). Moreover, the cultural turn
did not inherently entail greater attention to historical context.

---

[1] Much of the 'cultural turn' in development thinking that emerged in the 1990s derived from an
interest in the 'Asian Tigers', whose economic success prompted close (often paternalistic and
homogenising) examination of Asian societies to discern 'cultural factors' in their rapid growth
(Radcliffe 2006).

Kathryn Lafrenz Samuels (2018: 68–69) argues that the Bank embraced cultural heritage in response to the aforementioned criticisms of adjustment because it 'offered a lynchpin between bottom-up community development and the large-scale integrated development approach' that preceded it. Labadi (2022) suggests that this position was influenced by forces within UNESCO. In her analysis, criticism of development yoked to capitalism and consumerism was a significant part of UNESCO's policy from the 1960s to the early 1980s, with particular concern for protecting heritage from exploitation for tourism (Labadi 2022: 29, 36). Notable here is the tenure of Amadou-Mahtar M'Bow (to date the only African Director-General of UNESCO, 1974–1987), which included a strong emphasis on a vision of 'endogenous development based on cultural identity'. Echoing aforementioned positions by Ogot, Hountondji, and Odhiambo, this vision would be fulfilled through a combination of more robust cultural policies, enhanced educational opportunities (particularly concerning the arts and Indigenous languages), stronger implementation of UNESCO conventions and recommendations, and a 'bottom-up approach' to defining development projects (Labadi 2022: 32).

Some (but not all) resolutions advanced under M'bow's directorship were carried forward into the subsequent World Decade for Cultural Development (1988–1997), which promoted cultural diversity, co-operation, and human rights as prerequisites for economic progress via activities undertaken by UNESCO, its member states, and select NGOs (Labadi 2022: 37). Although the flagship publication for the Decade, *Our Creative Diversity*, suffered from a number of failings (notably, the lack of any new models of development based on diversity), the Bank and the UN Development Programme (UNDP) embraced its aims and translated these into financial support for cultural development projects. These included projects focused on the 'conservation and rehabilitation of tangible heritage and the safeguarding of intangible heritage' and, particularly within the Bank, on 'urban rehabilitation projects and projects aimed at generating revenue through heritage tourism and cultural tourism more broadly' (Lafrenz Samuels 2018: 73; Labadi 2022: 48).

Lafrenz Samuels (2018: 65) and Labadi (2022: 46–47) argue that this has resulted in heritage being co-opted in service of economic growth: rather than being 'mainstreamed' in development thinking, culture became an economic driver, which in turn meant that its value was subject to transnational commodification and privatisation (see Section 3). Heritage studies add a distinct perspective to literature reflecting on the dangers of uncritically promoting more localised participation in development (cf. Escobar [1995]: 2012). As communities have been drawn into participatory development schemes in cases like Morocco's Fez Medina and Mali's Djenné Djenno – wherein poverty is defined primarily in relation to heritage conservation, and local communities unable to fulfil a heritage management mandate become 'bad custodians' – their needs become cast in terms of present problems rather than long-term conditions (Joy 2007; Lafrenz Samuels 2009). This amounts to the sort of technocratic perspective broadly characteristic of developmental expertise (cf. Ferguson 1994; Bolin and Nkusi 2022), and when combined with the ambivalent position of the past within development's cultural turn, the result is a pernicious form of presentism.

1.4 Long-Term Strategies, Short-Term Tactics

With its economic value thus established, heritage was amenable to inclusion in strategies for long-term growth within African countries, but over the past three decades many of these strategies have succumbed to short-termism and a failure to account for entrenched systemic barriers. Historical perspectives on state thinking about culture for development illustrate how internationally-led heritage agendas conflict with domestic imperatives and lived realities (Jopela 2017: 150). For instance, Sierra Leone's 2014 national cultural policy was heavily influenced by *Our Creative Diversity* (drafting the policy began in the early 1990s). However, its focus on traditional practices exemplifying cohesion and non-violence was in direct contradiction with long-standing experiences of heritage performances like masquerade and the Freetown lantern parade, which do not necessarily support social unity:

> For every attempt to commodify some aspect of Sierra Leone's cultural heritage, or repurpose it for developmental goals, there is an equal demonstration of the recalcitrance of long-held cultural values and their ability to frustrate the intentions of state or international agencies. (Basu and Zetterström Sharp 2015: 57)

These processes are also at work in liberation and post-conflict heritage, where selective forgetting is frequently essential to nationalist narratives that are then affirmed by international development support from agencies like UNESCO, or from other nations via bilateral partnerships. In Mozambique, for instance, through the 'conservation principles and guidelines associated with the World Heritage system' the state has been able to strategically overwrite negative aspects of its civil war in favour of a unifying vision bolstered by a carefully crafted memory of liberation (Jopela 2017: 362). International aid for memorials commemorating the 1994 genocide in Rwanda (supplied by the UK, the United States, Germany, the Netherlands, and Sweden, among others) supported a moral stance on peace-building while reaffirming visions of a reformed nation restored to order and (by 2005) eligible for debt relief (Ibreck 2013). Memorials represent one of several arenas – including 'shared heritage' with Germany and repatriation of cultural property – in which selective framings of heritage as, inter alia, conciliatory, transnational, and precolonial bolster Rwanda's assertions of sovereignty in foreign policy relations (Giblin 2017b; Bolin 2021).

West African sites associated with the transatlantic slave trade are a particularly poignant instance of tension between experiences of heritage and the expectations of development. The early 1990s saw the United States Agency for International Development (USAID) and the UNDP funding the restoration of Cape Coast and Elmina Castles in Ghana. Plans to promote socio-economic development by increasing revenue from what has been termed 'roots tourism' or 'homegoing' drew protest from African diasporans opposed to modernising these structures and thereby commodifying sites of trauma (Osei-Tutu 2002). Restoration projects sat alongside others aimed at commemorating the transatlantic slave trade (for instance, UNESCO's 1994 Slave Route Project, incorporating other West African sites) and establishing events like the Panafrican Historical Theatre Festival (1992) aimed at attracting African American tourists (Engmann 2020).

Rachel Ama Asaa Engmann (2022) has detailed the complex heritage dynamics of these initiatives, which include blackface performances and monuments to slave merchants located on UNESCO's Slave Route in Benin (Araujo 2012). Meanings and experiences of the coastal fortifications are notably varied among diasporans and Ghanaians. For some, these constitute 'a secular pilgrimage to an ancestral homeland associated with transgenerational trauma' (Engmann 2022: 203). For others, they are archaeological and architectural historical sites attesting to centuries of economic and cultural activity, in which the transatlantic slave trade was one feature among many. These places also represent set pieces in the historiography of a post-colonial nation-building project focused on pan-African unity and progress. Ultimately there is, as Engmann (2022: 204) describes, a 'painful irony': development through this form of heritage tourism 'is based on a global capitalist system that, in previous centuries, commodified people themselves through the transatlantic slave trade and slavery'; the tourists/pilgrims in question here are themselves the descendants of that same system.

1.5 The Heritage of Betterment

While pairing heritage and development can thus complicate experiences of the past, the ahistoricism embedded in many neoliberal programmes and facilitated by their successors frequently disables critical examination of the antecedents of development programmes, and particularly of their status as heritage. By this, I mean the material and cultural legacies of long-term interventions aimed at upliftment that have been present on the continent for over a century and that shape the values attached to the past. Decker and McMahon (2020: 3–5) have described a 'development episteme' (ways of knowing about Africa with a view to improving conditions of living therein) encompassing missionary, extractivist, and scientific activities, as well as SAPs and beyond. The ways in which these earlier interventions aimed at engineering moral, technological, and commercial improvement has been the subject of numerous historical and anthropological studies – as has the capacity of those who were 'improved upon' to answer back (e.g. Comaroff and Comaroff 1991; Landau 1995; Meyer 1999). The material aspects of this long history of upliftment – the traces that it has left and how these have affected successive, related ways of thinking about and practicing betterment – have been less examined.

Missionary activities – and mission stations in particular – are perhaps the most obvious places to address these legacies. Work focusing on the material properties of mission demonstrates where we can access complex and transnational understandings of projects aimed at moral and economic improvement. Southern Africa has seen an intensive amount of research into the material, intellectual, and spiritual engagements that missionisation entailed, with studies examining missionary attempts to instil a morality expressed through specific visions of economic and domestic life (rectilinear homes, gardens, sedentary agriculture) (Landau 2000; Elbourne 2003; King and McGranaghan 2018; Mahashe 2019). Zoë Crossland's (2014: 88–89) study of Welsh missionary encounters with the Malagasy leader Radama I (r. 1810–1828) is noteworthy for charting how missionary characterisations of Radama's policies as socially progressive entailed reconciling observations of non-Christian practices with their standards of bourgeois morality. Missionary collecting practices – with artefacts circulating globally between colonies and the metropole – illuminate histories of benevolent paternalism, with displays of objects from the field casting missionaries as exalted figures and Christianising projects as worthy of global financial support (Wingfield 2018).

Moral upliftment was not the sole prerogative of missionisation under imperial conditions: scientific programmes aimed at improving the productivity of colonies and their residents illustrate how ostensibly technical approaches to development were coupled with personal and ideological sensibilities. Johanna Zetterström-Sharp (2020) has argued for an approach to legacies of imperial withdrawal that considers the personal social worlds of technical experts, their policies and practical interventions, and the effects of these on shaping post-colonial futures. Taking as her point of entry the archive of one British agricultural scientist and surveyor in Sudan during the 1950s and 1960s, Zetterström-Sharp (2020: 298) describes how private life coloured the ways that 'scientific truths' about landscapes, populations, and new technologies were formed and carried forward into post-independence planning. Perceptions of the 'cultural fragility' of southern Sudanese communities led to the assumption that rapid development would cause profound social turbulence; this in turn resulted in the 'regionalization of agricultural productivity', which was 'central to the way in which Sudan's future agricultural landscapes were imagined and financed' (Zetterström-Sharp 2020: 297, 295).

That scientific knowledge reflected the partialities and contingencies inherent in all colonialist projects is well established, particularly concerning African land and landscapes (Leach and Mearns 1996). Equally well established is how these knowledges endure where they are not systematically dismantled. Soil erosion has been a particular, recurrent concern over the last century in the eastern African savannah. Irrigation interventions have often been fleeting, and failed to take cognisance of resilient intergenerational strategies for landscape management, as Matt Davies and Henrietta Moore (2016) have observed among communities in Marakwet and Pokot. In Tanzania's Kondoa district, for instance, British policies of soil management based on the belief that African residents were overgrazing livestock were carried through to the post-independence period. Decades of interventions ensued, based on what were ultimately incorrect understandings of erosion's root causes (Lane 2009).

These observations bring to mind Frederick Cooper's (2010: 9) caution that while it is possible to retrospectively group missions, railroads, and so on into a *longue durée* of development, imperial governments maintained ambivalent, contradictory, or outright negative views of 'colonial development' policies. Approaches to development as heritage accommodate these shifting attitudes by highlighting how the legacies of modernising interventions represent varied visions of the future and, ultimately, varied temporalities. We can see this especially in instances where interventions aimed to uplift fall short of their intended effects or have impacts beyond what their instigators envisioned.

1.6 The Heritage of Failure

We can look to the heritage of failure to understand more fully the scope of development interventions and the intergenerational experiences of the people thus 'bettered'. Even where projects designed to improve peoples' standard of living have failed in their aims, they could nevertheless affect 'how social and political life is conceived and organised' (Piot 2010: 160).

The situation of pastoralists living in the Lake Turkana area illustrates these dynamics and their dimension as heritage. There, national and international schemes have promoted irrigated agriculture and an extensive fishing industry as solutions to food insecurity among nomadic communities. Premised on static and generally ahistorical understandings of pastoralist lifeways, successive development programmes encouraging irrigation cultivation and mixed agriculture beginning in the 1960s 'have regularly met with catastrophic failure' (Derbyshire 2020: 96). From the early 1970s, the Norwegian Agency for Development Cooperation (NORAD) invested heavily in a series of co-operatives tasked with acquiring and processing fish for sale in external markets, providing fishermen with new equipment like fiberglass boats and pouring upwards of US$20 million in a fish-processing plant and its connecting roads. While the scheme functioned more or less as intended during the 1970s, the disastrous installation of the processing plant (which could not generate enough energy to freeze fish proved financially unfeasible), drought, and the breakdown of several co-operatives under accusations of corruption heralded the collapse of NORAD's fisheries programme (Derbyshire 2019).

The material and organisational infrastructures representing the failure of development projects have been re-contextualised through use and memory. In Turkana, the roads NORAD built facilitate participation in a more flexible and better-networked (and therefore more sustainable) fishing industry encompassing Kenyan and Congolese fishermen. Boats and other remnant infrastructures enable a new system of trade in dried fish whose transport is better-suited to the fluctuations in demand that characterise Turkana's environment. In Kenya's Cherangani Hills, deforestation under various landscape management regimes was followed by forest preservation programmes that entailed multiple evictions of local Sengwer and Marakwet communities, creating a landscape scarred by destruction (Lunn-Rockliffe 2020). The result has not been the restoration of an ecological baseline, but the creation of new ecologies and livelihoods. Some of these (e.g. cattle grazing) are illicit under prevailing conservation regimes but necessary for survival amidst the constraints of overcrowding around the forest block. Development's failures are therefore intergenerational, as is resilience in response to these failures.

As we reflect on the ways development and heritage together shape (or overwrite) peoples' relationships to the past, we should remain alive to where heritage studies have allied the field to development through a shared commitment to the future (e.g. Basu and Modest 2015: 8). However, we have seen that development's future orientation is a product of neoliberal thinking. Heritage thus offers us an essential historical perspective for evaluating the truisms and values that neoliberal interventions encourage us to take for granted.

2 Heritage Governance in a Neoliberal World

Given that neoliberal policies have entailed reshaping and scaling back African states, how has heritage been implicated in these processes? African nations have been varyingly imagined and constituted for millennia, with the borders that emerged (or were imposed) at independence constraining imagined possibilities for new governing entities. Moreover, the relatively short period between many states achieving sovereignty and then having that sovereignty scaled back under SAPs makes the role of heritage in asserting national identity at home and abroad all the more noteworthy. Finally, amidst charges that donor conditions for financial aid were more concerned with achieving stability than democratisation, the view from heritage shows us where neoliberal interventions have excelled at preserving specific aspects of residual colonial administrations while purporting to do the opposite.

Indeed, as structural adjustment's scaling back of the state created a field into which non-state actors have crowded, the prerogative of the state to manage its patrimony has been ever more narrowly defined. The result is one of the many ways in which neoliberal projects contradict themselves and become apparent through heritage: heritage management apparatuses remain the purview of government structures while heritage practice is pulled in community-focused directions under interventions by activists, practitioners, and non-governmental actors from UNESCO to grassroots entities.

2.1 (Im)Mobilising the State in Africa

2.1.1 Rights to Rule from the Deep Past

Social complexity in Africa's long past took myriad forms beyond that of a hierarchical, centralised entity empowered through legitimated force and consolidated material wealth – to broadly sketch how we might characterise early statecraft thanks to Max Weber and his interlocutors (Pitcher et al. 2009). Of course, we need only look to the Sahara and southerly savannah in West Africa to see that hierarchical organisations did emerge from at least the first millennium AD, connected with extensive exchange networks and with social relations expressed spatially in urban centres (Monroe and Ogundiran 2012). But looking elsewhere – to the Great Lakes, the Ethiopian highlands, the Zimbabwe Plateau, and (not least) the middle Nile – illustrates the range of expressions for what David Schoenbrun (2021: 8) has termed 'groupwork': the practices of 'imagination' and 'assembly' through which communities have come into being.

Accounts of how the deep-time politics of African communities were transmuted or distorted into colonial and post-colonial states have implicated several phenomena: the ability of imperial administrations to perpetuate real and imagined forms of African statecraft; the colonial instantiation of technologies of power that would ultimately constitute post-independence exploitation and violence; and access to a vocabulary of legitimacy that was recognisable to constituents across multiple eras of governance (Bayart 1993; Mbembe 2015; Mamdani 2018 [1988]: 42–43). Where these trends coalesced into the view of neoliberal economists that African leadership was burdened by an inheritance of self-interested 'big men', Thandika Mkandawire (2015: 568–569) argues that this represents a fatally flawed understanding of the interface between tradition and modernity. This extensive literature from political science and economics has involved minimal engagement with the archaeological record. Trans-disciplinary *longue durée* treatments of political innovation through kinship ties, bushcraft, and cattle-keeping are therefore welcome innovations (Landau 2010; de Luna 2016; Jimenez 2020).

Visions of precolonial, distinctly African political forms also appeared in the philosophies of liberation thinkers and leaders like Kwame Nkrumah, Julius Nyerere, and Leopold Sédar Senghor, linking socialist aspirations to cultural inheritance (Adi 2018). These were core to liberation movements across the continent, even if unity proved difficult to achieve. West, Central, and eastern Africa all saw experiments in federation-building aimed at articulating new forms of sovereignty: rather than nation-states, regional co-operatives sharing distributed legislative and economic responsibilities (Cooper 2008). Even where actualised, though, these and any elements of state-making were frequently constrained by the fact that colonial states were incomplete, abnormal states whose governing infrastructure was dedicated to controlling the flows of people, goods (largely exports), and other resources between the colony and the rest of the world – what Cooper (2002: 5–6) has called 'gatekeeper states'. These were not designed to be sovereign, yet they bequeathed their apparatuses of rule to independent nations with the expectation that such nations would function in ways that they were never intended to (Young 1994). The peri-independence years in many African countries, then, were characterised, inter alia, by the residual burdens of colonial government, new imaginative horizons for what an African state could be, and global expectations of sovereignty.

2.1.2 Re-making the State at Home and Abroad

Development and heritage were two arenas in which new states could make ideologies of cohesion and progress concrete. Ultimately histories of European state creation held sway over ideas of 'proper' statehood during transitions to independence. These became the global standard for diplomatic and economic relations in the post-war period (Clapham 2001). As territorial nation-states materialised across the continent during the 1960s, ideologies coupling development with nationalism became a feature of the first generation of African leaders – in keeping with contemporary modernisation theory in development economics, and in contrast to later neoliberal narratives that vilified African states as incapable of prioritising social welfare (Cooper 2008).

Contemporary heritage nationalisms supported the role of states as forward-thinking providers for a unified citizenry. Major public heritage projects bolstered the legitimacy of political leaders and national cohesion, especially where these extended liberation ideologies. Kodzo Gavua (2015: 101) has described how Ghana's early governments 'established a tradition of monument building, naming, and renaming that has been fraught with subjective definitions of Ghana's heritage', rendered visible in the competing ideologies of Nkrumah's Convention Peoples' Party and opposition leaders like J.B. Danquah and Kofi Busia. Across the continent these monumentalities were part of a selective process of commemorating pasts that could best serve the cause of unification. For instance, Karega-Munene (2014: 27) suggests that Kenya's heritage legislation (updated ahead of independence in 1963) erred in granting protections for pre-historic rather than historic resources, as the focus on the former ultimately impeded the creation of a representative national identity.

Heritage preservation allied with development to constitute an arena for the 'new internationalisms' that characterised the 1960s and 1970s, where participation required not only demonstrating sovereignty but giving that sovereignty heft in the form of bureaucratic infrastructure that was legible to donors, lenders, and investors (Huber 2020). The promulgation of the 1972 World Heritage Convention entailed new possibilities for diplomatic manoeuvring under UNESCO's auspices. These occurred in multilateral settings like the World Heritage Committee (comprised of States Parties representatives and tasked with listing World Heritage sites), as well as networks of technocratic experts in heritage preservation and administration. The story of Lalibela's 1978 World Heritage inscription demonstrates how engaging with these networks required nations to adopt internationally recognisable language, institutions, and bureaucracies, while also validating particular national histories. This resonates with long-standing observations that post-independence African leaders were compelled to perform sovereignty in various international spheres as a condition for recognition and the benefits flowing therefrom, with consequences for (often dissonant and highly contested) authority at home (Clapham 1996).

Heritage also facilitated opportunities for states to imagine sovereignty within international solidarity movements. The Nubian Monuments Campaign to rescue archaeology affected by the Aswan High Dam (which saw its heyday in the 1960s and 1970s) illustrates these dynamics especially well. While UNESCO's ability to facilitate co-operation among participating states was variable, the campaign created a sphere of diplomacy and investment which allowed newly independent nations to bid for global influence and for solidarity organisations to navigate new alliances. Members of the Non-Aligned Movement (a relatively loose organisation of nations adopting neutral geopolitical positions during the Cold War) like Kuwait and India contributed monetary and archaeological resources to Egypt. These interventions varyingly supplanted, co-existed with, or enabled superpower interventions – thereby demonstrating how world heritage constituted a field that resists description within Cold War binaries (Carruthers 2022: 216–217, 220–224).

The question of whether or in what configuration African states could 'survive' was particularly acute where independence gave way to authoritarian rule and violent conflict. Where historians and political scientists have described this trajectory as the ascendance of 'neopatrimonialism', it is offered as evidence of the comparative weakness of leaders and their command of governing institutions (but see Pitcher et al. 2009). Again, though, international recognition was essential for the endurance of states even where these were widely condemned as illegitimate. During the 1950s–1970s, for instance, the French civil service and the European Commission's development programmes were both staffed by administrators with personal and professional ties to former colonies. These relationships helped perpetuate recognition of and dialogue with leaders like Uganda's Idi Amin and the Central African Republic's Jean-Bédel Bokassa even once their crimes had become apparent, although in a very few cases (e.g. Bokassa's) European Economic Community assistance was ultimately terminated (Dimier 2014: 112–113).

2.1.3 Roll-back and the Morality of Bureaucracy

In concrete terms, we can consider rolling back the African state under structural adjustment as achieved through three broad processes: fiscal constraints, fragmenting and limiting state control over public money, and stripping the state of (especially industrial) assets through privatisation (Mkandawire 2001: 307). As discussed in Section 1, development thinking in the 1980s emphasised government failure as the reason for slow or negative socio-economic progress. Constraining the state became a core principle of conditions on aid funding, with African states posing an acute problem: instability discouraged investment and therefore prevented markets from functioning as they should, meaning that a minimalist state was key to unleashing market forces (Ndulu 2008). From here, the narrative is familiar: NGOs, aid, and private investment crowded in to fill the role of the state, replacing local governance with technocratic solutions (Ferguson 1994). The 1990s saw a softening of this view in favour of assisting states to function better as co-ordinators, tasked with connecting opportunities offered by donors and investors (Harrison 2004: 18). Citizen cultures and the right to make demands on the state were, however, fundamentally reshaped (Kamat 2014).

While these measures highlight tensions between sovereignty and development, 'leaders have proven quite adept at side-stepping the ever-changing demands of international financial institutions – at least when it comes to their personal interests and control' (Cooper 2010: 18). Financial institutions have largely been unable to stop corruption and graft in national economies, and global security institutions were mostly toothless in the face of ascendant authoritarian regimes in (for example), Kenya, Cameroon, Chad, and Rwanda during the 1990s (Bayart 2000). While superpowers like the United States advocated for multiparty elections and good governance, the Clinton administration (like its predecessors) prioritised stability over democratisation and continued supplying aid to nations whose leaders had clearly eschewed the latter (Schmidt 2018: 333–338).

While the state may have been redeemed in the Sustainable Development Goals era, in many contexts on the continent its morality is still rendered dubious through rhetoric and action – a habit that has been reaffirmed in heritage studies. The rise of the grassroots as agents of participatory change ultimately aligned with paradigm shifts in heritage management and discourse: these emphasised 'bottom up' heritage values as a corrective to the long-standing dominance of a preservationist focus on monumental culture (Filippucci 2009). Heritage scholarship has overwhelmingly taken the grassroots as a study site, with the result that huge swathes of state administration have remained under- or un-studied (King 2019). This neglect of how bureaucratic cultures work to constitute impressions of sovereignty and legitimacy means that we risk missing an opportunity to understand how the state is surviving in practice and imagination among those charged with delivering on its functions. As Ferguson (2006: 38) has detailed, if neoliberalism's redistribution of governance means that we can no longer assume the state is 'up there' in a hierarchy of authority, then states and leaders have had to work harder or differently to perform their legitimacy and status.

As the rest of the section demonstrates, heritage has long been an active technology in constituting this 'up there' condition, particularly when state powers were qualified under SAPs but also in other, more recent contexts. At the same time, internationalisms oriented around liberation heritage and expanded global heritage principles illustrate where sovereignty and citizenship are constantly negotiated.

2.2 Persistence and Patrimony

Adjustment and its long aftermath often had devastating consequences: inequality widened, growth was slow, states were left with limited abilities to deliver core services that would ensure the welfare of their citizens (see Section 1). Adjustment was also fractured, contingent, and contradictory, often about preservation as well as change and frequently beyond the control of those who sought to manage it (Fredericks 2018: 5). The notion that 'neoliberalism's ostensible project of political streamlining provided surprising opportunities for the survival of state institutions and expanded mandate for some state employees' (Chalfin 2010: 9) is unexpected only if we accept that neoliberal interventions are monolithic juggernauts, replicating the same phenomena wherever they land.

I suggest that global standards of heritage preservation join technologies like customs duties as 'forms' that 'can be decontextualized and recontextualized, abstracted, transported, and reterritorialized, and [...] designed to produce functionally comparable results in disparate domains' – what Latour has called 'immutable mobiles' that become visible as a mode of global connection (Collier and Ong 2005: 11). Heritage administration on the continent has functioned as an immutable mobile where legislation and policy were implemented as part of colonial governance, and where their persistence (despite neoliberal restructuring) supports the axiom that 'most contemporary societies remain governed by yesterday's administrative structures' (Hansen and Stepputat 2001: 29–30).

Overall, the administrative history of heritage on the continent is arguably one of persistence rather than retreat. It is important to be clear about the tensions at work here: where legislation continued to vest the state with the power to manage patrimony, even where the *practice* of heritage management was qualified or enervated the *prerogative* to manage the national estate could remain nominally intact.

Historically, cultural and natural heritage protections tracked the state of research and discovery in their respective colonies, and in the early twentieth century these measures promulgated value systems that emphasised tangible, monumental heritage (Manetsi 2023). Where this legislation established heritage management bureaux and was little-changed by successive governments, we can see one mechanism whereby the administrative apparatuses for heritage remain relatively unreconstructed. For instance, Tanzania's Antiquities Act (established in 1964) was meant to replace the colonial Monuments Preservation Ordinance of 1937 but retained most of its provisions, which established the Division of Antiquities and its Directors as the chief decision-making custodians of (especially) tangible heritage in the country (Kiriama 2021). Ahead of its 1963 independence Kenya revised its heritage preservation and museum trusteeship ordinances with minimal changes to decision-making and appointment processes. This 'resulted in a stasis in terms of policy, capacity-building and heritage management' and meant that by 1968 the highest-ranking African at the National Museum was a ticket clerk (Karega-Munene 2014: 26). The Rhodesian government passed a string of nineteenth- and twentieth-century laws aimed at protecting monumental sites and rock art, the last of which (the 1972 National Museums and Monuments of Rhodesia Act) was adopted 'almost verbatim' as the National Museums and Monuments of Zimbabwe Act. This legislation vested the National Museums and Monuments of Zimbabwe as trustees of the nation's monuments or relics, a situation that interfaces with other legislation governing land acquisition and brings heritage in dialogue with territorial boundaries (Chiwaura 2009: 19–20).

Some restructuring is notable and has decentralised authority to an extent, in line with trends toward devolution of power explored in Section 3. Kenyan legislation passed in 1983 and subsequent governmental reorganisations have delegated powers of approval for heritage research permits to other ministries and district offices (Karega-Munene 2014). Legislation following significant regime changes – for example, Rwanda's 2003 constitution and 2016 law on the Preservation of Cultural Heritage and Traditional Knowledge – has created new positions and lines of accountability, as well as (in the case of Rwanda and Burundi) introducing stronger protections for intangible heritage and Indigenous knowledge (Kiriama 2023: 18). Alternatively, though, Uganda's Historical Monuments Act (acknowledging Western and traditional management) was issued under the first post-colonial administration in 1967 and was enhanced by the 1995 Constitution but not supplanted (Kamuhangire 2005).

Heritage governance was subject to the neoliberal pressures described previously through deliberate interventions curtailing support for the administrative state, which led to reduced resources for managing heritage centrally. Scott MacEachern (2001: 868) describes how decreased funding under SAPs led to the closure of Cameroon's Institut des Sciences Humaines, whose artefact collections were then used to fill potholes. In Morocco and Tunisia the withdrawal of the state from social services and the international dysfunction left in the wake of neoliberal policies enabled 'moneyed interests' and 'market forces' to over-extend the field of heritage into areas like poverty alleviation (Lafrenz Samuels 2018: 77). In Uganda SAP-induced cutbacks that reduced capacity for managing government archives dovetailed with co-ordinated nationalistic efforts by both the Museveni and second Obote governments to 'sever [. . .] state archives from national life' (Taylor 2021: 539).

NGOs have not only filled in where the state was absent but also have represented a forum for articulating visions of heritage excluded from definitions of national patrimony, particularly where these foreground Indigenous, community, intangible, or otherwise 'close to the ground' heritage that has been omitted at a national level (Karega-Munene 2014: 38). Kenya's community peace museums illustrate this particularly well. These emerged in the 1990s with funding from the Ford Foundation (among others) to foreground Indigenous peace-building traditions in response to conflict associated with the 1992 elections. Peace museums promoted living and multi-vocal heritage more than the focus on archaeological and palaeontological assets that dominated national institutions (Hughes 2014).

Notably, though, the general trend has been for states to retain their prerogative to control much of their national estate – which is core to any notion of sovereignty (I will return to some notable exceptions). In some cases this aligned to a strategic engagement with structural adjustment, as when Mozambique's ruling FRELIMO party instigated economic liberalisation measures in 1987 ahead of a formal SAP. This required Joaquim Chissano's government to pursue a heritage strategy that redefined the birth of the modern nation in terms of 'mozambicaness' instead of socialism, thereby making the state appear more amenable to privatisation (Jopela 2017: 282–284).

Heritage also constituted an arena in which (particularly authoritarian) leaders exercised their power, even when under pressure from democratising or peace-making interventions. Zimbabwe remains a poignant example of this. The invocation of liberation struggle veterans as literal and symbolic combatants on the side of Robert Mugabe's ZANU-PF has effectively extended the 'temporality of the liberation heritage' (Jopela 2017: 244): veteran heritage as enacted by the Zimbabwe Fallen Heroes Trust has constituted an emotive arena of public commemoration, as well as government-sanctioned evidence of ZANU-PF's historic right to rule (Mataga 2019; Fontein 2022). The Third *Chimurenga* of the early 2000s, with its cultural nationalist rhetoric invoking land, heritage, and anti-colonial resistance, constituted a rejection of neoliberal democratic ideologies and a bid for renewed ZANU-PF authority in the face of government's failure to deliver economically (Ndlovu-Gatsheni and Willems 2009).

The varied ways in which heritage sovereignty was challenged, defended, and adapted as African states were restructured make these bureaucracies significant sites of knowledge- and value-creation (King 2019). The position that institutions charged with heritage protections have occupied especially during periods of precarity for state power make them all the more important 'sites of neoliberal reason', where value systems and ideologies of rule are produced and negotiated even when governance is dispersed (Fredericks 2018: 6).

2.3 Latter-Day Heritage Internationalisms

While African states have generally preserved the rights (if not the resources) to manage their national estates, two internationalisms are worth considering where they qualify state sovereignty: the development of globally oriented heritage assets and the formation of liberation heritage networks.

Where heritage sites have constituted part of an internationally funded development project, states have been compelled to acknowledge global standards for managing these in order to comply with conditions on financing. Under these conditions, many African countries have had to build administrative capacity for supporting environmental impact assessments (EIAs) which often affect cultural heritage legislative and policy protections (Kiriama et al. 2010; see Section 4 for more details). For instance, the central heritage protections commission in Nigeria was established in 1977 but the Federal Environmental Protection Agency (constituted by the Environmental Impact Assessment Decree of 1992) retains oversight of EIAs. Where these assessments have encompassed heritage, regulatory review has been a dispersed, often un-coordinated series of overlaps between a patchwork of departments and committees (Awonusi and Aliyu-Mohammed 2010). Important to note here, then, is that the rise of heritage management spurred on by building works has compelled state and parastatal administrations to redirect their resources towards compliance measures and to take on the role of regulator. I return to this in Section 4.

We can see a similar process at work in the Operational Guidelines for UNESCO World Heritage sites, where the management practices and values at work are led by a multilateral agency but implemented by the state. Within this arena the prevailing approach has been that 'international cooperation is the only way to ensure effective long-term conservation of heritage and development of respective communities', placing relationships among States Parties and between States Parties and donors at the heart of any such undertaking (Jopela 2017: 157). However, and following George Abungu (2016), we should be careful not to confuse these dynamics for uncritical acceptance of outside guidance.

Anthropological studies of the World Heritage Centre – and especially the World Heritage Committee – demonstrate that this has long been a forum for diplomacy, with heritage protection one agenda item among many. World Heritage Listing has proven to be a venue for countries to exercise influence and manipulation, particularly where this involves States Parties overriding the recommendations of expert bodies like ICOMOS (Liuzza and Meskell 2023). Since at least the early 2000s the BRICS countries (comprising Brazil, Russia, India, China, and South Africa until the group's 2023 expansion) have formed a major bloc on the World Heritage Committee, 'using formal and informal influence to enhance their soft power' and protect one another from having sites placed on the List of World Heritage in Danger (Bertacchini et al. 2017: 345; see also Meskell 2014).

The result is a situation in which domestic heritage agendas are often at odds with international ones. Writing of his expertise with the World Heritage Centre, Albino Jopela (2017: 154) has argued that the dynamics described previously, alongside the challenges faced by state administrations at home, encourage African governments to 'opportunistically adopt a conservation strategy based more on advocacy for international donor funding and less on domestic measures that would empower local actors'. Jopela's criticism distinguishes between seeking international support for *existing* World Heritage properties and for establishing new ones: under the latter strategy states can access more resources by taking on responsibility for managing more heritage sites, even where there is not enough local infrastructure or capacity to sustain these. Akinwumi Ogundiran (2014) has described similar dynamics at work in the context of Nigeria's Osun-Osogbo sacred grove.

Questions of territorial and international heritage sovereignty take on different dynamics among African nations engaged in cross-border projects commemorating liberation struggles. As described previously, these movements were transnational and fuelled the establishment of contemporary solidarity organisations – not to mention tensions within and between these. The late 1990s and early 2000s witnessed the proliferation of multilateral programmes commemorating liberation heritage. Perhaps the most prominent of these is the *Roads to Independence: African Liberation Heritage Programme* instigated by Tanzania in 2003, encompassing eleven other southern African countries, and eventually endorsed by UNESCO. Following Jopela (2017: 195, 227), this and similar schemes in the region facilitated co-operative arrangements among partner countries and 'broadened the recognition' of contributions from countries seen as having weak liberation credentials (e.g. Eswatini and Botswana). These were also opportunities to smooth over internal regional conflicts, like the complex and contradictory position of Malawi's Hastings Banda as he aligned himself varyingly to the Southern African Development Coordination Conference (SADCC) and South Africa's apartheid government. South Africa has granted national heritage status to sites associated with other countries' liberation (e.g. the Samora Machel Memorial and Crash Site, relevant to Mozambique) and also repatriated the remains of the Herero King Michael Tjiseseta, a significant figure in the Herero Wars and their associated genocide (1904–1908), to Namibia.[2]

---

[2] Case 5632. Accessed 12 June 2024, available by request http://sahris.sahra.org/za.

While the dynamics just described are somewhat removed from adjustment interventions described earlier in this section, they are worth considering where they represent an ongoing reaction to those same interventions. Resourcing for managing national heritage estates has a direct bearing on a state's strategic engagement with international organisations like UNESCO. Liberation heritage represents a discursive and programmatic arena in which governments positioned as the successors to freedom movements can 'respond to changed circumstances' (Jopela 2017: 315).

2.4 Neoliberal Grassroots

While the instability and dysfunction of African nations became tenets of structural adjustment, these tropes are (as we saw in Section 1) ahistorical. Rather, the view of states as regulatory problems instead of historical entities is a symptom of a neoliberal framework, which an approach to heritage enables us to scrutinise against lived experience.

This scrutiny allows us to examine where the boundaries between the local and the central, the popular and the bureaucratic are far from clear. Of course, it is well established that the grassroots are fundamentally political and that technocratic approaches to heritage management – indeed, development more broadly – obscure local political processes and histories (Winter 2013). Heritage custodians have long been criminalised and silenced by states and their heritage apparatuses, from colonialist charges of occult activity to more recent evictions (Ndoro 2001). Participatory development schemes have had to contend with dangerous and dysfunctional relationships between the state and people who have been caretakers of heritage places for generations (Chirikure et al. 2018).

At the same time, many of these schemes have also made the interface between the grassroots and the state a site of both knowledge clashes and production. The involvement of traditional leadership and initiatives to widen participation in culture for development programmes illustrates this particularly clearly (Schmidt 2017). Relationships between traditional leaders and their constituencies can be contested terrain, made particularly problematic where abuses by the former have been implicated in widespread, long-term violence. Sierra Leone we see an example of a nationally led (but globally influenced) cultural heritage policy in which programmes aimed at empowering local participation in heritage run counter to chiefly authority – itself a protected heritage institution (Basu and Zetterström-Sharp 2015). Similarly, historians of development have been rightly sceptical of assuming too-rigid distinctions between the local and the 'up there', experts and non-experts, and also of the axes that these polarities create. The careers of African intellectuals who were commissioned to provide expertise to institutions like UNESCO on how to manage heritage sites – for example, Akalework Habtewold, Ethiopia's Minister of Education and Fine Arts, the first African President of the UNESCO General Assembly (1960–1962) – complicate efforts to critique 'Western experts' as a stand-in for other intellectual and practical interventions (Huber 2020: fn 25). Meanwhile, 'communities' can easily be mythologised by ruling elites to provide an alibi for continued power (Cooper 2010). Examining the heritage of the state thus implicates a wider topography of power – and encourages a more expansive purview for heritage studies within that topography.

3 Capitalising on Heritage

What does heritage entrepreneurship look like in neoliberal Africa? And, how does the treatment of heritage as capital inflect the relationship between individuals and collectives? I use the first question to attempt an answer to the second. Within these questions lie a number of entangled concepts and histories: changing configurations of citizenship and communalism; the complexities of defining heritage as something of value in a capitalist system; and persistent ideologies holding the authenticity of the past in tension with its public nature. I walk through these problematics to lay out why heritage entrepreneurship is significant lens for understanding the contradictions and (more often) the ambivalence of heritage as something to be marketed, rented, and profited from.

3.1 What Kind of Good Is Heritage?

Where heritage is valued as capital, scholars have consistently warned that local stakeholders will become increasingly estranged from the asset in question – its substance and its associated narratives.

This warning reflects an understanding of heritage as fundamentally communal rather than individual. Even where aspects of heritage depend upon obscurity for survival (e.g. Mokoena 2017), this still implies that a collective with a stake in that obscurity exists. The community is such a fundamental analytic within heritage studies that its subjective status has been roundly critiqued and qualified, even while values of community engagement have become a core to heritage practice (e.g. Waterton and Smith 2010). This analytical and conceptual emphasis on the community has meant that critical attention to heritage-as-capital – and particularly to where heritage is subject to monopolisation or enclosure in order to ensure profit – tends to draw sharp contrasts between heritage communities and entrepreneurs. The latter are usually considered as lone actors or corporations (e.g. Hall 1995; González 2014). Especially in the context of tourism, the work of nation-states and development experts in promoting economic growth through marketing heritage has been amply covered, as we saw in Section 1.

David Harvey's (2002: 94) discussion of monopoly rent is relevant to illustrate where tensions arise as a result of another fundamental feature of heritage as a marketable good: claims to authentic or unique qualities. Monopoly rent 'arises because social actors can realize an enhanced income stream over an extended time by virtue of their exclusive control' over something 'which is in some crucial respects unique and non-replicable'. There are contradictions here: the good in question can't be so unique as to resist a monetary value *but* the more easily it is marketed, the less special it becomes. Neoliberal economies should, in principle, resist monopolisation of any sort in order to keep markets flowing. As such, the challenge is 'to keep economic relations competitive *enough* while sustaining the individual and class monopoly privileges of private property that are the foundation of capitalism as a political-economics system' (Harvey 2002: 97, emphasis original). To that end, Harvey (2002: 101) identifies incentives for capitalists to promote 'local developments that have the potential to yield monopoly rents' – such as initiatives boosting community identification with, production of, and authority over heritage – even if these developments create or fuel an antagonistic relationship between communities and capitalists.

These claims to uniqueness or authenticity beg further questions: does uniqueness relate to *actual* or *perceived* scarcity (i.e. scarcity created discursively)? We can also ask, to what extent does this tension between local actors and capitalists hold up as global trends in communication and transport have made it increasingly difficult to maintain spatial boundaries around assets (a point that Harvey [2002: 98] makes)?

Further, the innovations of a liberal marketplace means that heritage-as-capital takes a number of forms that remain to be sufficiently examined. Particularly significant in this Section is what I refer to as 'derivative heritage', borrowing from Bram Büscher's (2010: 261) 'derivative nature' and referencing the broader category of financial derivatives – perhaps best-known as the products that fuelled the 2008 global financial crisis. For our purposes, derivatives are 'representations of value' bought, sold and invested in separately from or instead of their underlying assets: museums whose existence (with or without reference to their collections) function as a basis for influence brokering; ecotourism offerings promoting connections between rural people and nature while visions of actual poverty are carefully stage-managed; and so on. Thinking with derivatives and other financial specifics gets us beyond a discursive view of heritage commodities to something that markets actually work upon and with.

We can now consider a useful framing of heritage-as-capital while indicating aspects in need of further resolution. First, despite widespread insistence that international flows of capital have re-defined or blurred the distinction between the global and the local, those distinctions nevertheless remain within the frameworks just described (Thrift 2006). Second, much of the existing literature does not help us get very far in imagining entrepreneurs as located *within* 'local communities'. Third, while authenticity and scarcity are characteristics produced discursively, it is still incumbent on us as critical analysts to scrutinise the realities of how those values are produced. Discourse still requires labour, risk, and materials.

3.2 Heritage, Inc.

Where heritage scholarship has had the most to say about the commodification of identity and culture, this has focused on situations that can be described as autonomous or 'grassroots' – led by a particular constituency invoking their own heritage and asserting its authenticity through proximity to the local or the traditional. The assumption is that in marketing a communally held cultural feature one of two things happen: either a community identifies more intensely with the culture being commodified as market consumption takes off, or they enter 'a Faustian bargain of sorts' resulting in 'self-parody and devaluation' (Comaroff and Comaroff 2009: 12). Regardless of the outcome, heritage entrepreneurs are held liable for the inevitable fault lines between those who gain and lose from commodification, even where states bear some responsibility for encouraging this sort of scheme through its own rhetoric and economic strategies (Meskell 2012: 41). This is to say nothing of more cynical forms of exploiting, mythologising, and 'Disney-fying' African pasts already subjected to long histories of denial or obfuscation (Hall 1995; Hall and Bombardella 2005).

That said, we need only look to examples like Paulla Ebron's (1999) study illustrating how corporatised heritage experiences – in this case, homegoing tourism mediated by McDonalds and elided to the 'Roots' television series – are sites of meaning-making on a personal and collective level. More recently, arenas of public life hitherto seen as inappropriate for commodification are increasingly treated as fair game for profit-making (Jethro 2020: 147–148, 152). Not to mention the fact that 'grassroots players' can engage with the commercial and non-commercial values of heritage simultaneously, without the one negating the other (Hughes 2018: 183). Indeed, while it has been relatively easy for heritage scholarship of all stripes to label something or someone as buying in to 'Heritage, Inc.', these ascriptions rarely lead to in-depth considerations of the varying conditions of capital and enterprise involved (Peterson 2015).

There is also room to expand upon the intersection of entrepreneurship and citizenship. A vast body of literature on the latter has emphasised where creating political belonging in sovereign African states reflects a tension between moral and civil commitments: on the one hand, citizenship can constitute 'a domain of rights and duties' for addressing 'unequal social relations'; on the other, an individualist and largely amoral way of relating to traditional collectives (Ekeh 2004; Hunter 2016: 8). Across the continent, civil society has been a cornerstone of interventions promoting liberal democracy. When combined with economic empowerment schemes the result is a major trope of neoliberal thinking: the responsibilised citizen. Endowed with personal freedoms and given access to financial resources on an individual level (e.g. micro-credit schemes described next), the responsibilised citizen is accorded the power to make their own claims of both the state and the market, thereby creating their own successes – and failures (see, inter alia, Rose 1999: 142; Asad 2003: 157; Brown 2015 for discussions of this concept). Examining how heritage entrepreneurship works in practice enables us to navigate differences between responsibilised citizens and moral communities invested in putting the past to use.

3.3 The Art and Craft of Micro-finance

Programmes aimed at subsidising, training, and promoting artisans, craftspeople, and tour guides abound on the African continent, aimed at equipping people to profit from their knowledge of and proximity to heritage. Such projects are often yoked to other schemes invoking heritage for economic growth, especially tourism. These empowerment schemes constitute a genre of micro-investment in which the capital involved is capacity instead of, or in addition to, money and goods. Although the latter certainly happens, many heritage empowerment schemes appear more comfortable trading in knowledge than in cash.

This model differs from the more common permutations of micro-finance that have characterised generations of (ostensibly) socially responsive development economics. By the 1990s, revisions to the Washington Consensus and its hard-line neoliberalism included critiques of long-standing donor-financed micro-credit schemes: these were, it was argued, neo-colonial and created relations of dependency. New models wherein banks and private financial institutions provided small loans to individuals were presented as more efficacious: these would provide capital subsidies to the world's 'bottom billion' and thus enable the poor to generate income in previously inaccessible markets (Collier 2007; Roy 2010: 14–16). While micro-finance models vary regionally, their proponents have insisted 'that microfinance embodies a new moral paradigm in the economy of finance, what may be designated as "responsible finance" or "ethical capitalism"' (Roy 2010: 218).

A core issue here is the ability of the poor to take on debt and risk. The engine that makes these schemes function – the ability of capital backers to secure repayment or otherwise demonstrate returns on their investment – has been revealed through ethnography to be largely contingent upon a wide array of family and sociocultural factors. This is particularly the case where micro-finance schemes emphasise loans to women (Karim 2011).

These models do not lend themselves to heritage easily, although the Culture Bank model offers a clear example. The Fombori Culture Bank, founded in Mali in 1997, responded to instances of looting archaeological sites for sale in the antiquities market. Residents deposited objects in the bank, which kept and displayed them as security against small cash loans and training for 'income generation'. The scheme was hailed as a success and spread across Mali, and to Togo and Benin. It hinges on the convergence of the value of an artefact and the micro-credit loan, which has generated creativity and conflict alike among bank clients (Leloup 2021).

More commonly, micro-investment in African heritage entails subsidising human capacity and/or creative products. Here, economic risk inheres in introducing goods whose value derives from their special, 'authentic' quality into a consumer context that can easily affect that special-ness through mass production and substitution. We see this in, for instance, schemes to market traditional basketry made by women in communities associated with Botswana's Tsodilo Hills. Market demand ultimately compelled artisans to modify their practices to become less authentic and more widely appealing (Keitumetse and Nthoi 2009).

The misalignment of the service or craft on offer and the nature of the market in question has been a perennial concern in heritage tourism on the African continent (Snowball and Courtney 2010), and also speaks to connections between urban and rural poverty. Especially with initiatives to train and equip tour guides and stewards at rural heritage sites across South Africa, Sudan, Mali, and elsewhere, such schemes often reveal socio-economic and infrastructural blind spots (Joy 2010; Duval and Smith 2013; Morris 2014; Humphris and

Bradshaw 2017). Access to roads or other forms of transport and amenities like reliable electricity are necessities not only for a tourism industry but for basic well-being. In South Africa, for instance, efforts to promote tourism to rural areas (whether for traditional 'homestays' or to archaeological sites) confront the challenges of a limited, poorly resourced roads system. This is acute in former 'homelands', where the transportation infrastructure (or lack thereof) is a consequence of apartheid-era planning: roads were designed to regulate the movement of migrant labour and channel white South African tourists to hotels and casinos, thereby racially partitioning revenue streams (Rogerson 1990).

We can also note an overly narrow understanding of the economic landscape in heritage micro-finance, as rural incomes contingent on 'access to markets and technical support' have been highly variable across the continent (Becker and Frankema 2019: 209). Linkages to cities are particularly important in this context, although here as well investment in heritage capacity too often fails to reckon with its position amidst formal and informal economies. For instance, following a UNESCO programme for guides on the Island of Mozambique three out of six guides were able to 'move out of extreme poverty' while 'the one who did this to the greatest extent' had a network of financial support (Labadi 2022: 117–118). The scheme did not tap into markets or infrastructure sufficient to ensure enough tourism traffic to remain in business full-time. In this way, guiding as a small business venture becomes part of Africa's informal employment sectors. For optimists these sectors are hotbeds of entrepreneurial potential, particularly in urban areas where access to formal employment is uneven; sceptics point to the limited impact of financial investment in these contexts (Becker and Frankema 2019: 211).

Seen as one hustle among many, heritage-related ventures like guiding start to look more feasible on the understanding that they likely will never be a primary source of income. But this contingent, informal business is often incompatible with schemes that imagine guiding or similar undertakings as ultimately becoming self-sustaining. Even where capacity is treated holistically within a web of personal and economic relations it is now well-established that capitalising individuals does not inevitably uplift whole communities; women often bear the burden of this misalignment (Karim 2011). Labadi's (2022: 124) study of a training programme for Senegalese artisans at heritage sites demonstrates that this trend persists despite attention to social financing at multiple points in a long chain of heritage value.

Conversely, heritage authenticity can trump market-driven innovation, with dire consequences. For instance, over many years the masons (*barey-ton*) tasked with preserving Djenné Djenno in line with UNESCO guidelines have been prohibited from modifying their craft and raw material use. Forced to turn down commissions from Djenné residents wishing for more practical, economical housing facades the *barey-ton* have been constrained in their capacity for economic growth (Joy 2012: 62–64, 143–144). Djenné represents an extreme case in which heritage safeguarding directives limit the effectiveness of poverty alleviation measures as well as community-driven entrepreneurship.

3.4 Biocultural Entrepreneurship

The biocultural axiom – the premise that nature and culture are inseparable and mutually sustaining – emerged as a key element of the 1992 Rio Summit and provided the practical and conceptual connection between biodiversity (a cornerstone of ecological resilience) and Indigenous knowledge (the basis for stewardship that is viable in the long-term) (Vidal and Dias 2016).

Pairing biodiversity with Indigenous rights took on a particular trajectory in African countries where nation-building was premised on eliding cultural pluralism (e.g. Botswana, Tanzania). Asserting rights on the basis of identity frequently ran counter to these ostensibly liberal democratic projects (see, inter alia, Saugestad 2001; Kenrick and Lewis 2004; Barnard 2006 for discussion). Nevertheless, not only have sub-national identities proven key to experiences of citizenship (Smith 2013), but global support for Indigeneity as a language for making claims of government found a home within neoliberal civil society on the continent (Giblin 2017a). This produced a visible and profitable sphere of advocacy within nature conservation: tourism markets seized on the possibilities for a product in which the appeal of African nature could be made ethical by investing in associated Indigenous communities (Igoe and Brockington 2007).

Nature conservation is thus converted into capital, and takes an especially neoliberal turn when consumers are told that 'their only course of ethical environmental action is through consumption', and where those ethics implicate Indigenous and other stakeholder communities (Brockington et al. 2008: 196). The process of commodification goes further, however, where the value of conservation resides in the domain of the spectacle rather than actual on-the-ground materials, resources, and knowledge. Returning to Büscher's (2010: 272) 'derivative nature', we can see how 'investment in derivatives leads to the building of harmonious constructions of nature and poverty that become increasingly alienated from the actual natural environments and peoples they are derived from'. This chimes with Meskell's (2009: 94) description of the South African government's strategy for investing in wildlife parks: 'biodiversity is packaged as entrepreneurial, economically indexical, and global, whereas cultural heritage is backward-looking [and] politically fraught'. This exclusion of culture was a significant discursive strategy amidst the complex politics of restitution after the country's democratisation, but it also foreclosed a wider understanding of the rich histories of Black life in and around nature parks (Dlamini 2020).

Considering where culture *does* fit in to nature entrepreneurship, we could ask how such ventures articulate with, for instance, long-term moral entanglements within a political economy of rights, land, and resources. Perhaps the most well-researched examples of this work concern constituencies of Maasai in southern Kenya and Tanzania who have successfully built a global brand as 'iconic conservationists', promoting eco-tourism and support for Indigenous custodianship of the environment (Lane 2015). In both countries post-independence, Maasai have contended with persistent colonialist attitudes and policies treating pastoralists as responsible for rangeland degradation through immoderately grazing and stocking animals. 'Modernisation' schemes pressured Maasai and other minoritised ethnic groups to abandon transhumance in favour of more sedentary lifeways, coupled with large-scale relocations that often built upon colonial-era dispossessions (Boles et al. 2019).

Dorothy Hodgson (2011: 68–69, 157) has demonstrated how Tanzania's changing landscape of governance engendered through structural adjustment came with mixed results for nomadic communities. Decentralisation and privatisation in the late 1980s and 1990s reduced cattle inoculations against tick-borne diseases (leading to elevated cattle deaths) and increased 'illegal and quasi-legal incursions' into pastoralist territories by revenue-generating enterprises like wildlife parks, mines, and commercial farms. On the other hand, the expanding presence of NGOs aimed at promoting Indigenous rights created a political and discursive space in which pastoralists could make demands of the state. However, through the 1990s and 2000s localised and NGO-led efforts frequently ran aground against the challenges of coordinating these efforts amid government hostility.

During this period, advocacy for Maasai rights and economic empowerment focused strategically on an international audience, supported by NGOs, donors, and agencies who facilitated entry into a global tourism market favouring a particular vision of ethical consumption. Offerings in the Maasai Mara Reserve, for instance, combined safaris with visits to *manyattas* ('cultural villages'). Heritage is a significant part of these experiences, both in their marketing (leaning on a defined visual language featuring Maasai dress and material accoutrements against a savanna backdrop) and the role that *manyattas* play in curating and transmitting Maasai heritage (Lane 2015: 263–265). While numerous *manyattas* were created by Kenyan and Tanzanian community members looking to support employment and revenue creation, others are operated by hotels and tour companies who are alleged to take a significant cut of the profits.

These initiatives entail complicated dynamics between past lifeways and present livelihoods. It is well documented – particularly in eastern Africa but also elsewhere (e.g. Witz 2006) – that any enterprise whose value rests on deep-time sociocultural continuity (from dance troupes to 'traditional' village home-stays) can slip into reifying visions of timeless Indigeneity (Salazar and Zhu 2015). Whether tourism projects take this approach (hiding evidence of 'mod-ernity' in *manyattas*, not disclosing that Maasai are financial stakeholders) or opt for an experience that clearly indicates the connection between capital and local economic uplift, at issue is how the value of the experience on offer is defined. But, as Lane (2015: 278) has argued, 'laying claim to a heritage as conservationists' premised on deep-time continuities is a high-stakes strategy in Kenya and Tanzania, where this same rhetoric has been the basis for over a century of marginalisation, disenfranchisement, and violence against pastor-alist peoples.

3.5 Moral Entrepreneurship and Devolved Government

Heritage institutions can lend themselves to a different sort of enterprise: the creation of *political* as well as financial capital. This is a broader, more expli-citly social, form of entrepreneurship. It bears discussion for what it can reveal about how political and economic transitions directly implicate heritage in (re-) making moral communities. Instances where governments have been devolved or decentralised illuminate these processes. While this Element has thus far treated decentralisation more in terms of social service provision than territorial governance, here I address the latter more explicitly.

Federalism and decentralisation (distinguished by the former's constitutional provision for sub-national autonomous powers) in African states have been lauded internationally as facilitating more democratic and efficient governance. Among the features of these widespread transformations is the 'resurgence of traditional authority structures', whether formally through administrative pol-icies premised on ethno-linguistic identification (e.g. Ethiopia) or less formally through the daily interactions of state and local agencies (e.g. Nigeria). Conflict between these institutions is not uncommon (Erk 2014: 543).

Fundamentally, decentralisation creates space between the unit of devolved governance and the state in which entrepreneurs can move; heritage can serve as political and financial capital within that space. For instance, in 2010 Kenya's revised constitution devolved power to forty-seven counties. This created new administrative structures and funding streams along with opportunities for new local elites to emerge amidst changing leadership dynamics (Josse-Durand and Meckelburg 2022). Projects memorialising heroes and heroines of Kenyan liberation (Swahili, *mashujaa*) became associated with this period as a means of facilitating unity in the context of both devolution and the aftermath of widespread post-election violence in 2007/8 (Coombes 2014). These memorials also represented opportunities for socio-economic entrepreneurs to claim recognition, as was the case with the erstwhile Koitalel Samoei Nandi Trust. This proposed a mausoleum and museum honouring the eponymous freedom fighter from the Northern Rift Valley. Through these institutions and other measures (e.g. the 'Nandi Political Code of Conduct' initiative), influential businessmen and Nandi community leaders have leveraged a combination of political savvy and ancestral claims to stabilise the region politically and economically (Josse-Durand 2018).

Opportunities for participation in electoral processes are key to facilitating this sort of heritage-inflected dynamism. Ethiopia offers a contrast where the relatively limited opportunity for multiparty competition means that heritage institutions can offer expansive arenas for entrepreneurial manoeuvring. In 1995 Ethiopia implemented a federal system divided along ethno-linguistic lines. One way that the constituencies thus created could legitimate themselves was through displays of ethnographic material at (for instance) the museum established in Konso, southern Ethiopia. However, these moves have the potential to exacerbate conflict. Amidst tensions between national and clan authority, and expert and financial aid from organisations like UNESCO and the Musée du Quai Branly, entrepreneurs have succeeded where they could demonstrate their value as 'brokers' capable of navigating formal and informal administrations to deliver development outcomes. Chloé Josse-Durand (2015) follows one 'development broker' who receives 'commissions' (clothes for his family, a mobile phone, a moped) in return for purveying strategic information to experts and researchers. Referring us back to monopoly rent, Josse-Durand's work illustrates how entrepreneurship applies to whoever can most effectively communicate exclusive control over assets like strategic knowledge within a situation where local politics are obscured by the federalist state.

My arguments in this Section have been both discursive and practical, bearing on the relationship between heritage and particular marketplaces. As micro-credit initiatives, artisanal and guiding initiatives have a performative value that outweighs their profit in real terms. 'Derivative heritage' as a concept clarifies how tourism and expertise are monetised differently as discourse and lived experience. This is even before we consider situations where poverty itself is the commodity on offer (e.g. slum tours) and an uncritical market logic dictates that a business premised upon experiencing poverty will somehow remove its reason for existing (Giblin 2017c). There is a need to be precise as to whether the goal of these and, indeed, any enterprises capitalising on heritage is to use profit-seeking as a means of *safeguarding or generating* value: the former does not automatically lead to the latter and to assert otherwise without economic and ethnographic validation is to blindly accept neoliberal dogma that internalising values within a market system automatically makes them worth maintaining. Moreover, this critical perspective enables us to recognise clearly where neoliberal systems commodify things that were never meant to be commodified, with consequences that I describe in the next section (cf. Skosana 2019: 24–27).

4 Infrastructure and the Business of Preservation by Record

Infrastructure – from railways to dams, ports to agricultural facilities – has been key to planning for economic progress in African countries under colonial and sovereign regimes alike. While infrastructure can be broadly construed as facilitating movement across time and space (Larkin 2013), in the context of neoliberal growth infrastructures are crucial to ensure connectivity with global export/import markets and enable access to resources like energy, water, and telecommunications (Chalfin 2010).

Since the 1970s, a series of environmental legal and policy instruments have promulgated the polluter-pays principle, which recognises that infrastructure-building entails pollution and that managing this pollution creates a burden for states and citizens. The principle was enshrined as Principle 16 of the 1992 Rio Declaration in 'aspirational' rather than 'obligatory' terms intended to 'streamline economic approaches to environmental regulation' and encourage economic activities to be maximally sustainable (Schwartz 2015: 430; De Sadeleer 2021). Principle 16 originally envisioned the public sector as responsible for regulating environmental damage, but within the last three decades definitions of what counts as mitigation and who counts as a polluter have expanded: polluter-pays measures now empower markets to encourage things like carbon offsets and cap-and-trade programmes that 'green' the economy by delivering financial returns to investors (Schwartz 2015: 448).

Relevant to us here is that a polluter-pays approach became an animating force in development financing: the World Bank made assessing and mitigating environmental damage arising from its projects a key condition of funding since at least the 1990s as part of what Michael Goldman (2005: 50, 154, 205) referred to as its '"green neoliberal" period'. Through a number of other binding and non-binding instruments (including Principle 17 of the Rio Declaration and the 1991 Espoo Convention), assessing social and environmental impacts have become 'part of a state's due diligence' and ideally inform planning for development (Elias and Wong 2021: 189). However, the implementation of polluter-pays was originally concerned with environment as a biological and physical matrix; *cultural* heritage became incorporated into frameworks for managing impacts via different historical routes.

Imperatives to rescue monumental heritage threatened by infrastructure building have a notable history on the African continent: the Nubian Monuments Campaign is perhaps the most infamous instance of this (see discussion in Section 2). But the campaign was a moral, technological, and geopolitical exercise in global heritage making, and predated the global acceptance of polluter-pays standards (Allais 2013). Impacts on cultural heritage featured prominently in planning for development from the late 1980s, notably in standards for World Bank compliance like those just described but with a particular mandate: specifying protections for 'cultural patrimony' was a response to both an awareness of the scale of pollution and destruction at issue *and* a drive to make heritage pay financially (Cernea 2001). Over time, global norms for heritage safeguarding standards on development-financed projects have shifted: while IFIs enforced relatively universal compliance measures for much of the 1980s and 1990s, the last few decades have seen shift towards recognising host countries' sovereign frameworks for heritage management (see Section 5). Throughout, however, the influence of the polluter-pays principle has engendered a basic premise: that developers have a financial stake in mitigating the damage they cause.

The principle that capitalism can solve the same problems it creates by appropriately valuing the costs and benefits involved is a deeply neoliberal one, akin to carbon offsets in its conceptual and moral work (Buller 2022). As I detail next, at a methodological level mitigating heritage in the service of development – work that constitutes the cultural resource management (CRM) industry – involves conceptually carving up assets to evaluate their relative worth. The process is similar for ecological assets, and conservation ecologists have observed where imperatives to assign value to ecosystem features 'cuts up these connections and relationships in order to produce, sell, and consume the constituent elements' (Büscher et al. 2012: 8). While these observations pertain particularly to biodiversity – imbuing nature with 'profit potential' as an imperative to save it – the transformation from entangled value system to individually evaluated assets has long been a feature of mitigation strategies (King and Nic Eoin 2014).

Where laws and policies are crafted primarily with environmental impacts in mind, procedures for assessing impact and assigning value to threatened assets either treat cultural heritage as downstream from environmental considerations or omit it altogether. In the latter case, leveraging mitigation for cultural impacts involves extending environmental protections to heritage (Kiriama et al. 2010). But these frameworks obscure the fact that, while we accept that nature and culture are interlinked, heritage values are not coterminous with ecological ones. Moreover, the modes of conservation, preservation, and salvage available diverge widely depending on the sort of asset in question.

For monumental, architectural, and archaeological heritage the dominant mode of mitigation has been preservation by record: even where excavation or rehabilitation is called for, textual and visual documentation is almost universally regarded as an acceptable way of safeguarding value (Brusius and Rico 2023). Where preservation by record is the most-widely used methodology in CRM, this has had tremendous consequences for both the estates of many African countries and, ultimately, the question of how public culture is affected by developer intervention.

Here, I unspool the historical and contemporary bureaucratic red tape linking financial institutions, developers, national heritage authorities, and on-the-ground heritage managers within regulatory systems aimed at holding capital accountable for its impacts. I demonstrate how the nature of risk and (ultimately) knowledge associated with heritage on the African continent is contingent on the practices of infrastructure financing and development. The implications are wide-ranging, and I close by focusing on the changing roles of museums and archives as preservation by record is itself re-made.

4.1 Infrastructure, Development, Freedom

Realising the capital potential of African colonies depended upon extracting, processing, and exporting resources efficiently, and prior to World War II 'development meant the expansion of infrastructure' for these purposes (Decker and McMahon 2020: 107). Particularly in the inter-war years, invest-ment in railways, roads, and ports in British colonies served an additional 'social imperialist' purpose by, for instance, creating jobs necessary to produce railroad steel. Impelled by a series of strikes across African industrial sectors, the 1930s and 1940s witnessed the beginnings of French and British develop-mental agendas coupling infrastructure enhancement with support for African welfare. This was a shift from earlier positions that colonies should 'pay for themselves' and thus receive little investment beyond the necessities of keeping production on track (Cooper 1997: 65–69). This new developmentalism was codified in Britain's 1940 Colonial Development and Welfare Act (CDWA, extended in 1945) and France's 1946 Fonds d'investissements pour le développement économique et social (FIDES), with the latter claiming that infrastructural modernisation 'would integrate African communities into commerce' while maintaining their 'traditional' qualities (Cooper 1997: 70).

FIDES focused particularly on public works and infrastructure (65 per cent of funding from 1946 to 1956) while introducing mechanisms that produced persistent conditions of indebtedness. Colonial revenues were expected to match funds invested and colonies addressed shortfalls borrowing from the Caisse Centrale de la France d'Outre-Mer, which precipitated financial crises in, for instance, Chad. These relationships of dependency were 'perpetuated' and 'normalized by postcolonial loans from the World Bank and the IMF', along with private investments recoverable through international litigation (Decker and McMahon 2020: 139). Dubbed Britain's 'second colonial occupation' (Low and Lonsdale 1976), investment in infrastructure under the CDWA took the form of large mechanised projects like the Sukumaland Development Scheme (Tanzania) and the Tanganyika Groundnut Scheme, the latter requiring a purpose-built railway and a port at Mtwara; these were ultimately regarded as failures and became symbolic of the British Labour government's wider shortcomings (Hodge 2007: 209–213). On the other hand, schemes like the Kariba hydroelectric dam sought to eke out economic growth from British protectorates by placing industrial capacity in the hands of white settler minorities (in this case, the ill-fated Central African Federation of Northern and Southern Rhodesia and Nyasaland), who would then be responsible for facilitating African economic growth (Tischler 2013: 4).

African nationalist movements of the 1940s and 1950s and a renewed wave of strikes gathered momentum from dissatisfaction with post-war industrial development, which included unpopular land reforms seeking to increase production by privatising communal land (Hodge 2007: 224). Newly independent states in the 1960s and 1970s embraced industrialisation and expanded interventionist development activities both in the service of economic progress and also to demonstrate the effectiveness of the state in enhancing citizens' lives (Cooper 2002: 85–88, 99–100). Continuities between experts in colonial governments and international development agencies have already been discussed in Section 1, representing an extension of development thinking into UN agencies and institutions like the Bank and IMF.

4.2 Accounting for Heritage Impacts amid Neoliberal Reforms

While rescuing heritage from development became a global concern with the Nubian Monuments Campaign, the notion that impact mitigation was not only desirable but achievable as a condition of financial compliance became a feature of World Bank policy from at least 1986. In 1986, the Bank's operational policy OPN 11.03 codified 'do not harm the heritage' with respect to movable and built heritage (Cernea 2001: 29–30). OPN 11.03 clarified the Bank's non-assistance for projects damaging cultural heritage and laid out a range of options for mitigation (e.g. re-design, relocation). However, for much of the 1990s this translated into largely passive, reactive protection of chance finds (Cernea 2001: 30). Over time and with encouragement from precedents in the Middle East and North Africa, in 1999 the Bank embarked upon a new framework for action that endorsed (among other measures) proactively safeguarding physical cultural patrimony and embedding this protection in development objectives: for instance, using heritage as the basis for diversifying income generation in aid of poverty reduction (see discussion in Sections 1 and 3). The Bank has remained a world leader in cultural heritage policies among IFIs, even amidst the growing impacts of 'alternative' IFIs like the New Development Bank (NDB), the African Development Bank (AfDB), and others (see Section 5).

Alongside and occasionally intersecting with the Bank's evolution in heritage protection policies were its transformations in environmental and social protection policies. Some have characterised these as a response to criticisms of structural adjustment (e.g. Watts 2006: 44), although individual scandals also played a part. Following the 1990 disaster of India's Sardar Samovar Dam – where protests by villagers living along the Narmada River ended in police violence – and the negative findings of the Bank's first Independent Review Panel, the Bank committed to upholding sound environmental and social standards for their projects. This entailed imposing 'green conditionalities' that pressured 'borrowing states to establish and/or restructure' their environmental governance and regulation. Apparatuses of these states were re-made specifically to provide and service the environmental and social needs assessments that such loans demanded (Goldman 2001: 192–194). We saw in Section 2 how this affected state sovereignty. Here, it is important to note where policy revisions treated environmental and social impacts separately from heritage impacts.

Returning to the Bank's heritage policy, despite language insisting that heritage has non-economic value (Cernea 2001: 33), according heritage 'developmental value' imposed the expectation that experts and host states alike quantify the yields of its preservation (Lafrenz Samuels 2018: 66). Following Lafrenz Samuels (2018: 64), this 'created an institutional mechanism for managing archaeological remains and choosing actions for mitigation' which, as with 'green conditionalities' mentioned earlier, entrained states to providing relevant heritage management measures. Historically, this has taken the form of legislative or regulatory responses, public–private partnerships, or outsourcing expertise to contractors (see MacEachern 2010; Arazi 2011 and discussion herein).

The state roll-back described in Section 2 becomes relevant here: under SAPs states ostensibly retained the right to make some decisions about their patrimony but their administrative bureaucracies were constrained or selectively resourced. Heritage sovereignty, then, is contingent on both policy and practical capacity, as we shall see illustrated next. It is worth noting that in the early twentieth century the Bank moved towards a clearer statement of heritage sovereignty in development contexts: a revised Bank operational policy in 2006 (OPN 4.11) specifically recognised state authority over heritage management by stipulating that impacts on cultural resources could not contravene host countries' legislation or international treaty obligations. This position points toward a form of 'borrower control' over compliance that has become increasingly significant within the landscape of international development finance, and I return to it next.

4.3 Salvage Archaeology: An African Industry (Sometimes)

CRM operations in Africa have taken a variety of forms: from efforts by individuals or teams (e.g. Ghana's Akosombo Dam [Folorunso 2000], Sudan's Merowe Dam [Kleinitz and Näser 2011]), to limited or non-existent efforts (e.g. Côte d'Ivoire's Kossou Dam [Gachuruzi 2000], Ethiopia's Gilgel Gibe Dam [Brandt 2000]). Dam-building in newly independent nations from at least the early 1960s saw enhanced concern with national heritage protection and featured more sustained archaeological research, as with the Mono Dam between Togo and Benin and with the Akosombo Dam; the latter served as 'a catalyst for Ghanaian archaeology' as a professional field (Posnansky 2000: 36). More common, though, are instances where good-quality archaeological assessment and mitigation work have not been supported by appropriate financing or included in planning for large infrastructure, as Caleb Folorunso (2000: 33) has noted was the case with respect to Nigeria's Kainji Dam.

As Section 2 described, the 1980s and the advent of SAPs in numerous countries compromised the functionality of state heritage protection where they choked off administrative resources. Conversely, this same decade saw Mali and Botswana pass legislation instantiating a polluter-pays approach to heritage management and normalising archaeological impact assessments prior to construction (van Waarden 1996; Sanogo 2007). South Africa adopted similar measures in 1999. In, for instance, Sudan, Nigeria, and Kenya, legal protections for development-affected heritage have come from a combination of legal protections for the environment and cultural patrimony (compare UNECA 2005, Ndoro and Kiriama 2008, Kiriama 2021 for discussion of these have developed over two decades). Taken together, these protections represent an effort to place financial burdens for impact management firmly on developers.

Where compliance measures associated with IFI-funded projects filled gaps in national heritage protections, these frequently took the form of teams of international experts carrying out mitigation work, sometimes with support from African professionals but often not. Writing at either end of the first decade of the twentieth century, Scott MacEachern (2001) and Noemie Arazi (2009) drew attention to the lack of input from African professionals in setting heritage management priorities amidst the travelling expertise employed by international development institutions (cf. Lafrenz Samuels 2009). This is in spite of specific provision in Bank operational policy for heritage to actualise its economic value through building local capacity; more about this next. Arazi (2009: 96) particularly highlighted the potential for a heritage management industry to create long-term employment for African archaeological graduates. This potential has been realised patchily across the continent (Manetsi 2023).

At the same time, the involvement of international expertise – even where this is sanctioned by lenders – is not a guarantee of compliance. In a review of road-building projects, Arazi (2011) identified cases in Mali (Second Transport Sector Project), Ghana (West Africa Regional Transport and Transit Facilitation Project), Tanzania (Transport Sector Support Project), Senegal (Diamniadio Highway), and Uganda (Transport Sector Development Project) in which impact assessments were non-compliant with Bank operational standards – not least because they neglected to identify well-known and -documented archaeological sites – but nevertheless proceeded. At the same time, the literature is replete with examples of CRM programmes that received sufficient resourcing due largely to the intervention of a single committed person or group, as with Somalia's Bardheere Dam, where the USAID Mission Director was an archaeology enthusiast (Brandt 2000: 33).

Partly in response to dissatisfaction with governmental and conditional protections for heritage, archaeological organisations have attempted to set standards for practitioners across the continent with varying degrees of coverage and impact. The Nouakchott Call for Preventive Archaeology in Africa, initiated by the Mauritanian Institute of Scientific Research and France's Institut national de recherches archéologiques préventives is particularly notable in its insistence on applying the polluter-pays principle to heritage management (Naffé et al. 2007).

4.4 Heritage versus Development?

Neither the concept of polluter-pays (as a means of assigning culpability for industrial damage to the environment) nor the notion of salvaged heritage as an economic driver fully captures the range of heritage values that emerge through CRM. The Bank, for instance, has viewed the economic contributions of this work in terms of tourism and capacity building: through, for instance, site inventorying and skills provision the latter type of intervention has the potential to 'facilitate policy implementation' (recalling Goldman's 'green conditionalities') (Campbell

2009: 15–16). These values are exemplified (if not fully realised) in association with monumental, heavily marketed, sites like Uthina (Tunisia, Lafrenz Samuels 2008) or Lalibela (Ethiopia, see discussion in Section 1).

Across numerous development schemes the potential for heritage management to serve as a vehicle for capacity building has been limited by systemic failures to appreciate the nature of the capacities in question. Arazi (2009: 100) described Africa 2009 – a UNESCO-sponsored training scheme for heritage managers – hopefully while it was ongoing. Retrospective critiques have cited the programme's focus on replicating Western-led heritage typologies and management strategies that ultimately failed to advance novel practices specific to local needs (Ndoro and Wijesuriya 2015: 140). Arazi (2009: 96) also wrote optimistically of the New Partnership for Africa's Development (NEPAD), supported by the Organization of African Unity (OAU) as a co-ordinated effort to increase GDP and meet other health and social welfare milestones (Loxley 2003); NEPAD featured language recognising the role of heritage management capacity in this scheme. International aid funding provided through NEPAD, though, ultimately proved inadequate to its goals. While assessments of NEPAD's outcomes almost overwhelmingly exclude heritage, it is safe to assume that (as with other government sectors) this did not receive its hoped-for boost (Payne 2005: 163–164).

Failure to think strategically about capacity building is also endemic at project-level. For instance, in an ethnographic account of heritage management associated with the Chad Export Project, MacEachern (2010: 355) details the disconnect between the expertise of Cameroonian and Chadian archaeologists and the expectations of Exxon's bureaucracy concerning technical writing and bidding. Rapidly translating knowledge and proposals into the bureaucratic framework of a relevant development partner is a capacity that the Bank is well-placed to facilitate, but did not in the situation MacEachern describes.

While one may think of tourism and capacity building as outcomes of (particularly archaeological) heritage management, understanding the significance of heritage *in its own right* implicates still other value systems. Viewed one way, the archaeology at issue represents data at risk of loss, and mitigation involves recovering that data through various means: excavation, survey with or without collection, site recording, or a combination thereof. Archaeologists may sometimes prioritise data collection over preservation in situ, as I discuss shortly.

Development-affected communities have described how heritage impacts are not only material but social, financial, and spiritual, particularly where ancestral remains are concerned (Skosana 2019). Heritage practitioners have demonstrated where community-led approaches can mitigate the effects of socio-economic upheavals associated with (for instance) resettlement ahead of building projects. The situation at Ghana's Bui Dam remains the pre-eminent example of this potential (addressing concurrent community re-settlement and burial ground destruction; Gavua and Apoh 2016), while negative examples abound from the Omo-Turkana region (Clack and Brittain 2018) to Phases IA and IB of the Lesotho Highlands Water Project (LHWP, Thamae and Pottinger 2006; Kabi 2023) and beyond. The problem-atic execution of nominally mitigating measures has contributed to public dissatisfaction with industrial development and the business or government entities behind this (as at Sudan's Merowe Dam, Kleinitz and Näser 2011). At the extreme end of these consequences are court cases brought by mining-affected South African families whose ancestors were exhumed and reburied in ways that can only be described as traumatic (Esterhuysen and Scacaggi 2014). Following Rob Nixon (2011), infrastructure development represents a 'slow violence' that leaves few areas of life untouched while compounding existing and historical inequalities.

Ultimately, though, the economic value of heritage in the context of infrastruc-tural development has frequently been constrained by the *value of the infrastructure in question*. Although the Bank has maintained that it does not fund projects with substantial cultural heritage impacts, where it has financed a *sub-project* and its compulsory impact assessments therefore took place after work commenced, these 'survey and salvage' operations have been subject to a policy that 'every effort must be made to avoid project delays and contractor penalty payments' (as per a 2009 guidance document, Campbell 2009: 26). The same directives do not necessarily apply to developer-led work financed through other means, but where heritage impact assessments are required relatively late in the development process it is difficult to avoid seeing these primarily as potential obstacles – at least from the developers' and financiers' perspectives (Ichumbaki and Mjema 2018: 29–30). This necessarily inflects the heritage values at issue, compelling participants in the process to weigh these against the costs of delaying or halting building.

Heritage values in the context of development impacts are therefore multiple, unstable, contingent: preservation and progress exist neither in a mutually reinforcing relationship nor in a one-to-one trade-off. The galaxy of highly mutable, complex relationships enabled within these projects underscores the widespread consequence of a system in which assets are carved up, stabilised, and evaluated within a matrix of risk mitigation and benefit maximisation. Further, and building on Trinidad Rico's (2015) discussions of heritage at risk, we can recognise that the vulnerabilities at issue resist circumscription: mitigation measures that do not account for risks as systemic, mutable, and historically accumulated will always be in danger of being incomplete.

4.5 Structural Adjustments to the Archaeological Record

The archaeological record is a process of selectivity and destruction: excavation and related procedures target specific places and materials; they alter, de-contextualise, and/or demolish their objects of study and the data recovered are archived, accessioned, and transmuted into text and image. These records are therefore loci of 'translation between the material past encountered during excavation and the production of archaeological knowledge as an intellectual exercise' (Baird and McFayden 2014: 15). While in mitigation contexts 'preservation by record' is sometimes an alternative to excavation (particularly in the case of rock art and intangible heritage, Nic Eoin and King 2013; Arthur et al. 2021), this is not an alternative to destruction and still represents a site of knowledge production.

In African CRM and elsewhere, the relative quality of archaeological records generated through the 'discoveries' of antiquarians, through the targeted questions of researchers, and through development projects have been exhaustively debated. A theme in a 2007 volume on CRM in Francophone Africa is the potential for CRM to overcome historical and contemporary sampling bias: archaeologists may not be the primary decision-makers in these contexts, but the spatial and financial scale of development projects often permits more data collection in a wider area than academic projects could manage (Naffé et al. 2007). This perspective exists in tension with approaches to mitigation whose first recourse is to avoid heritage impacts entirely, as was the case on Exxon's Chad Export Project, in which (local and Western) archaeologists argued for *more* excavation rather than re-routing building work (MacEachern 2010: 357–358). Here and elsewhere in West Africa (e.g. the dams along the Volta River, Posnansky 2000: 36), CRM represented perhaps the best opportunity to gather information that was otherwise inaccessible due to the complexities and expense of conducting large-scale work.

By contrast, Merowe Dam illustrates that in well-studied areas with long population histories the issue isn't *more* archaeological data collection but rather *different sorts* – namely those of immediate relevance to development-affected communities. Ahead of a new dam at the Fourth Nile Cataract in Sudan, local communities rejected an archaeological salvage mission because archaeologists were insufficiently attentive to the socio-economic and heritage priorities of people immediately impacted by the dam. In this and other situations in which communities were invited to describe their priorities for mitigation, these included graves, homesteads, environmental knowledge, personal and family histories, and places related to oral narratives, among others (Kleinitz and Näser 2012; Gavua and Apoh 2016). At Merowe these priorities emerged in direct conflict with those of some archaeologists, while at Metolong Dam (Lesotho) they were foregrounded through an intangible heritage mitigation programme that framed its remit around the question of 'what heritage will local people lose access to?', rather than 'what archaeological data are worth retrieving?' (King and Nic Eoin 2014). Operational definitions of loss and risk shape the available approaches to mitigation.

In the aggregate CRM projects outnumber academic ones and cover more ground, although the archaeological records they generate are more often contained in reports than in published material. Approaches to curating these reports vary widely: South Africa and Namibia have launched open access digital repositories; in some cases museums (e.g. Kenya), national archives (e.g. Sudan) or parastatal agencies (e.g. Zimbabwe, Botswana) are responsible for storage; consultants may retain their own materials without publication; or developers may embargo publication of any data (e.g. the LHWP's Phase IA and IB dams). This uneven availability represents a problem in terms of the knowledge that these documents contain: if CRM is responsible for an ever-larger share of the archaeological record, and given that archaeology relies on contextualising information to interpret the past, what does it mean when such vital, vast information is patchy or inaccessible?

CRM has also reshaped knowledge about the past by reshaping the institutions responsible for managing that knowledge. In addition to the relevant records, the objects, samples, and sometimes individuals recovered during salvage operations require curation and care – typically by museums. The curatorial crisis afflicting museums worldwide is especially acute where provision for accessioning and storing materials from CRM work is generally limited, with CRM generating more material than museums can manage. The constraints on this storage capacity rarely (if ever) constitute grounds for modifying the scope of a CRM project, meaning that the pipeline from development to mitigation to storage is flowing at an almost overwhelming rate (Kersel 2015; Childs and Benden 2017; Brusius and Singh 2017).

This is especially relevant as museums across the continent are asserting a distinctly forward-looking place in community life. Initiatives in (for instance) Ghana and Zimbabwe are exploring innovative curatorial and co-creative practices that invite museum communities to imagine how objects associated with the past can speak to 'local ontologies' and sustainable futures (Ayim 2021: 6; Chipangura and Mataga 2021). However, where curatorial capacity is consumed by managing volumes of material generated through CRM activities, it raises questions about whether these management obligations are compatible with other museum agendas, or where they siphon away precious resources in order to look after a constantly growing body of material. Of course, this latter undertaking is essential to ensuring knowledge about the past is not lost; the point is that it is necessary to understand how it articulates with other priorities within institutions tasked with looking after heritage and how these institutions are staffed, funded, and granted authoritative input in planning for future progress.

5 Neoliberal Legacies

This Element has laid out a methodology for interrogating how neoliberalising agendas and heritage practices have shaped each other within a distinct historical context. This approach is especially useful because heritage and culture have been invoked ambivalently or inconsistently (and sometimes not at all) in development policies over the last few decades (Labadi 2022: 2), meaning that searching for a straight line between a policy and its manifestation in heritage practice is often a frustrating endeavour. But where heritage *has* been made to work in the service of governance or socio-economic improvement this is neither accidental nor a downstream consequence of 'market forces' (Meskell 2012: 39). Connections are there, but forged in the complexities of the personalities, institutions, histories, and geographical circumstances involved in the cases described in this Element. Indeed, this is one reason why the perspective offered here is necessary: neoliberal ideas have been institutionalised, contested, and hybridised with other technologies of progress in ways that vary widely in time and space. Where heritage becomes a site for this sort of creative work we can learn something about how it is implicated in producing features of the world that we take for granted.

Among the insights available from this approach is the ability to disentangle the epistemic and moral preoccupations behind calls to make the past pay. Under the financial and governance conditions of the 1990s and early 2000s, imperatives to put the past to work through tourism and other modes of cultural production were a feature of government, NGO, and aid rhetoric and policy. This is, however, neither the first nor only time that publics, lawmakers, financiers, and scholars have called for using the past for urgent, relevant projects in the present: from nationalisms to visions for the future of African historical, philosophical, and archaeological studies to popular culture productions and beyond (see King forthcoming for a review). An uncritical, generalised perspective on neoliberalism would treat *all* efforts to put the past to work as more of the same relentless march towards valuing everything within a market-driven system. The historical work done in this Element helps to locate value and public benefit within different – and differently entangled – backstories, and to be precise about where commitments to neoliberal development persist in peoples' lived experiences (Wiegratz et al. 2018) and into more recent development incarnations like the Sustainable Development Goals (Gabay and Ilcan 2017). There is an intellectual imperative to trace these in order to be precise about the futures we imagine.

Relatedly, this Element demonstrates the significance of holding to account those who have impeded or failed to deliver on promised futures. Foregrounding the heritage of development and insisting on a role for the past in socio-economic planning are powerful ways of countering the in-built ahistoricism of neoliberal development. This becomes apparent once taken-for-granted aspects of heritage for development within a wider field of vision. Heritage studies would therefore do well to return to exhortations by Eisha Odhiambo and Paulin Hountondji and ask: how can heritage provide insight into the calls for endogenous development that emerged as the neoliberal order has become entrenched, and that remain resonant in heritage management (Abungu and Ndoro 2022)?

With this in mind, I describe two key areas in which neoliberal legacies laid out in this Element have serious implications for the future of heritage on the African continent.

5.1 Heritage Sovereignties in the Era of Alternative Development

Over the past two decades, alternative development financiers have been edging the BWIs out of their position of global primacy. Recalling discussions previously about the conditions that the World Bank imposed on its financial support, lenders like the NDB, the AfDB, the Islamic Development Bank, the Southern Africa Development Bank, and China's major overseas banks have adopted a 'country systems' approach to compliance: put simply, lenders defer to the host country's legislative and regulatory protections for managing social and environmental impacts caused by development. A country systems approach recognises host countries' sovereignty and promises more 'borrower control' over investments, as opposed to institutions applying a uniform set of regulations to all their investments and loans.

However, where lenders do not establish minimum standards for social and environmental safeguards and where national provisions for these are weak, impacts can be mismanaged (Ray and Kamal 2019: 211). A 2015 AfDB review concluded that none of its member countries possessed in-country capacity to assess and implement these necessary protections, particularly concerning involuntary re-settlement. History has shown that heritage impacts are especially high and difficult to manage when development projects cross national and sub-national boundaries (MacEachern 2010). This is relevant where investment heavily favours the transport and telecommunications sectors: since 2018 the former has been a major focus of Chinese lending to African countries (Ray 2023: 2), and the World Bank's Private Participation in Infrastructure database (which tracks private investment, including sovereign wealth funds and private equity) has shown the latter among the top three growth industries in both sub-Saharan and North Africa for the last two years.[3] Moreover, the current trend among private and Chinese state-led financing is towards a large number of relatively small-scale projects, which can have significant heritage impacts but are challenging to track, resource, and address within building works that are typically fast-moving, as Elgidius Ichumbaki and Elinaza Mjema (2018) have shown.

Many lenders do have safeguarding standards, but comparative analyses of operations in Latin America have shown that these are variable in their criteria and requirements for disclosing the details of impacts (Gallagher and Yuan 2017). This is concerning in view of a geospatial analysis of China-financed projects between 2008 and 2019 (including those within China's Belt and Road Initiative, launched in 2013) demonstrating that, globally, 63 per cent of these projects overlap with critical habitats, protected areas, and Indigenous lands; in Africa risks to Indigenous lands are most extreme in Mali, Mauritania, Morocco, Niger, Nigeria, Chad, Ethiopia, Egypt, Gabon, and Namibia (Yang et al. 2021). This overlap has, however, decreased between 2018 and 2021.

Following the trend described in Section 4, heritage is rarely (if ever) accounted for in meta-analyses of impacts, but the significance of the afore-mentioned trends is clear. Section 4 described the variability of systems suited to pre-development assessment and mitigation for heritage across the continent, and where heritage protections are often afforded via provisions within *environmental* laws and policies. Moreover, Section 2 described where state and parastatal heritage management has been enervated by decades of restructuring and restricted spending, and where domestic heritage priorities can be subor-dinated to international ones in (for instance) the case of World Heritage properties. At issue is not just the future of heritage itself but the rights, livelihoods, and well-being that accompany development: following Lane et al. (2016), where development-affected communities have negative or trau-matic experiences of heritage salvage these frequently pre-figure displacement or alienation from the benefits promised by (for instance) dams and roads. A key issue here is how heritage-worth-saving is conceptualised within mitigation programmes, and the need for legal frameworks and professionals alike to

---

[3] PPI Visualization Dashboard, Infrastructure Finance, PPPs, and Guarantees, World Bank. https://ppi.worldbank.org/en/visualization, accessed 27 November 2023.

address the conflicting issues raised in Section 4: is the purpose of CRM in development contexts to generate income, preserve the past, or address the needs of impacted people (King and Nic Eoin 2014)? Each of these has different policy implications, meaning that precision in language and concepts is key, particularly within national standards for safeguarding.

5.2 Cultural Property in the (Sort-of) New Digital Commons

Section 3 demonstrated where entrepreneurship exists in tension with the premise that heritage is fundamentally communal. This unresolved tension is bearing fruit as questions about the commodification and digitisation of cultural property have become increasingly urgent.

Intellectual property (IP) rights related to African cultural heritage have been a recurrent source of anxiety and conflict over the last several decades. Regional multilateral organisations like the SADCC featured discussions about IP protections in its conferences on cultural protections in the early 1990s: the SADCC was specifically concerned to protect African material and visual culture from expropriation in a globalising world (King 2019). High-profile controversies like patenting San knowledge of the plant *Hoodia gordonii* (Foster 2018) and Disney's efforts to trademark the phrase 'hakuna matata' (first in 2003, again in 2018) demonstrate where IP rights intersect with persistent bio-colonialism, extractivism, and global financial inequality. The Hoodia case in particular shows where cultural IP can be protected based on a proprietary claim by a community – in this case by an *Indigenous* community – with support from multilateral treaties like the Convention on Biological Diversity.

But, as Ancila Nhamo and Seke Katsamudanga (2022) have demonstrated, two issues are crucial for sustainably and equitably commercialising heritage in the future: ownership and utilisation. Following Nhamo and Katsamudanga (2022: 80), laws governing national heritage in African countries overwhelmingly reflect the view that heritage is held by the state in trust for the nation and *not* by individuals. These laws are therefore aimed at 'registering and providing protection and conservation' to sites, objects, and archives and are premised on the notion that the point of heritage management is preservation for a common good rather than utilisation for limited gain. In some countries (for instance, South Africa, Kenya, Cape Verde, Madagascar, Mauritania), provision does exist for legally protected heritage to be used in service of socio-economic development but with few specifics of what this entails beyond the familiar tourism-conservation or microfinance models described in Section 3.

Of course, heritage can be proclaimed and marketed independent of what governments say. And there are good reasons for the protections just described, particularly given the past and present of looting and the trade in antiquities on the continent. The point here is: where there is a desire to commercialise heritage while simultaneously (1) protecting this from appropriation and (2) ensuring that gains (financial and otherwise) from commercialisation go to specific beneficiaries, it is essential to have legal clarity on who has the right to derive profit from heritage. This is key to the functioning of creative industries and to patenting traditional knowledge for medicinal purposes (among other examples), and some countries already have enabling legislation. For instance, in Congo-Brazzaville, Eritrea, and Ethiopia, legal protections allow national heritage to feature in commercial productions. In Egypt, Uganda, and Malawi, heritage is categorised as a form of cultural property for purposes of fostering the growth of cultural industries (Nhamo and Katsamudanga 2022: 75–78).

Legal protections for IP in African countries are salient in the widening context of generative artificial intelligence (AI). These issues are too recent and fast-moving to have received much coverage in heritage scholarship, but artists like Malik Afegbua have embraced AI art generation, while also raising concern about where AI technology appropriates artists' work without permission or credit (Habte 2022). At the same time, as African languages are under- or un-represented in the datasets used to train language learning models, initiatives have emerged to populate existing datasets with these languages or create alternatives (Ojo et al. 2023). But, as Indigenous language enterprises elsewhere have illustrated, providing speech data to large multi-national companies risks losing control of both the context of those languages and the financial gains derived therefrom, as datasets may be sold on or otherwise mined for commercial opportunities (Coffey 2021).

This technology is innovative, but, as described previously, concerns over heritage and IP have been pervasive (if under-acknowledged) for decades. They ultimately trace back to the ambivalence surrounding heritage entrepreneurship: how does monetisation affect relationships between individuals and communities, particularly when enterprise rests on an understanding of ownership and profit that may not easily fit the heritage in question? This Element has laid a foundation for understanding how questions of use and ownership have been shaped by the financial flows of the last thirty years, enabling more nuanced responses to the increasing diversification of heritage commodification.

Abbreviations

AfDB	African Development Bank
AI	Artificial intelligence
BRICS	Brazil, Russia, India, China, South Africa (I use this acronym throughout, acknowledging that the bloc's membership has expanded beyond these countries.)
BWI	Bretton Woods Institutions
CDWA	Colonial Development and Welfare Act
CRM	Cultural resource management
FIDES	Fonds d'investissements pour le développement économique et social
FRELIMO	Frente Libertação de Moçambique
GDP	Gross domestic product
ICOMOS	International Council on Monuments and Sites
IFI	International financial institution
IMF	International Monetary Fund
IP	Intellectual property
LHWP	Lesotho Highlands Water Project
NDB	New Development Bank
NEPAD	New Partnership for Africa's Development
NORAD	Norwegian Agency for Development Cooperation
OAU	Organization of African Unity
SADCC	Southern African Development Coordination Conference
SAP	Structural adjustment programme
UN	United Nations
UNESCO	United Nations Educational, Scientific, and Cultural Organization
UNDP	United Nations Development Programme
USAID	United States Agency for International Development

References

Abungu, G. O. 2016. UNESCO, the world heritage convention, and Africa. In *A Companion to Heritage Studies* (eds. W. Logan, M. N. Craith, and U. Kockel). Oxford: Wiley Blackwell, pp. 373–391.

Abungu, G. O. and W. Ndoro 2022. Introduction: The heritage of the colonized. In *Cultural Heritage Management in Africa: The Heritage of the Colonized* (eds. G. O. Abungu and W. Ndoro). London: Routledge, pp. 1–10.

Adi, H. 2018. *Pan-Africanism: A History.* London: Bloomsbury.

African Development Bank Group 2015. *Assessment of the Use of 'Country Systems' for Environmental and Social Safeguards and Their Implications for AfDB-Financed Operations in Africa.* Abidjan: African Development Bank Group.

Akyeampong, E. K., R. H. Bates, N. Nunn, and J. A. Robinson 2014. Introduction: Africa – the historical roots of its underdevelopment. In *Africa's Development in Historical Perspective* (eds.A. Akyeampong, R. H. Bates, N. Nunn, and J. Robinson). Cambridge: Cambridge University Press, pp. 1–29.

Allais, L. 2013. Integrities: The salvage of Abu Simbel. *Grey Room* 50: 6–45.

Apoh, W. 2013. The archaeology of German and British colonial entanglements in Kpando-Ghana. *International Journal of Historical Archaeology* 17: 351–375.

Araujo, A. L. 2012. Transnational memory of slave merchants: Making the perpetrators visible in public space. In *Politics of Memory: Making Slavery Visible in the Public Space* (ed. A. L.Araujo). New York: Routledge, pp. 15–34.

Arazi, N. 2009. Cultural research management in Africa: Challenges, dangers and opportunities. *Azania: Archaeological Research in Africa* 44 (1): 95–106. https://doi.org/10.1080/00671990902808179.

Arazi, N. 2011. Safeguarding archaeological cultural resources in Africa: Policies, methods and issues of (non) compliance. *African Archaeological Review* 28: 27–38. https://doi.org/10.1007/s10437-011-9090-8.

Arthur, C., P. Mitchell, L. Mallen *et al.* 2021. Record-making, research, and removal: Mitigating impacts on rock art in a CRM context in southern Africa – the case of the Metolong Dam, Lesotho. *African Archaeological Review* 38: 675–694. https://doi.org/10.1007/s10437-021-09464-4.

Asad, T. 2003. *Formations of the Secular: Christianity, Islam, Modernity.* Stanford: Stanford University Press.

Awonusi, F. S. and A. Aliyu-Mohammed 2010. The state of impact assessment and heritage and management of heritage in Nigeria. In *Cultural Heritage Impact Assessment in Africa: An Overview* (eds. H. Kiriama, I. Odiaua, and A. Sinamai). Mombasa: Centre for Heritage Development in Africa, pp. 28–34.

Ayim, N. O. 2021. Editor's introduction. In *A New Chapter: Ghana's Museums and Cultural Heritage. Presidential Committee on Ghana's Museums and Cultural Heritage.* ANO Institute of Arts and Knowledge. https://ghana-heritage-future.s3.eu-west-2.amazonaws.com/Museum+Report+(v.3).pdf, accessed 17 November 2023.

Baird, J. A. and L. McFayden 2014. Towards an archaeology of archaeological archives. *Archaeological Review from Cambridge* 29 (2): 14–32.

Barnard, A. 2006. Kalahari revisionism, Vienna and the 'indigenous peoples' debate. *Social Anthropology* 14 (1): 1–16.

Basu, P. and W. Modest 2015. Museums, heritage, and international development: A critical conversation. In *Museums, Heritage and International Development* (eds. P. Basu and W. Modest). London: Routledge, pp. 1–32.

Bayart, J.-F. 1993. *The State in Africa: Politics of the Belly.* London: Longman.

Bayart, J.-F. 2000. Africa in the world: A history of extraversion (trans. S. Ellis). *African Affairs* 99 (395): 217–267.

Becker, F. and E. Frankema 2019. Poverty in Africa. In *Routledge International Handbook of Poverty* (ed. B. Greve). London: Routledge, pp. 203–216.

Bertacchini, E., C. Liuzza, and L. Meskell 2017. Shifting the balance of power in the UNESCO World Heritage Committee: An empirical assessment. *International Journal of Cultural Policy* 23 (3): 331–351.

Boles, O. J. C., A. Shoemaker, C. J. Courtney Mustaphi *et al.* 2019. Historical ecologies of pastoralist overgrazing in Kenya: Long-term perspectives on cause and effect. *Human Ecology* 47: 419–434. https://doi.org/10.1007/s10745-019-0072-9.

Bolin, A. 2019. A country without culture is destroyed: Making Rwanda and Rwandans through heritage. Unpublished doctoral thesis, Stanford University.

Bolin, A. 2021. The strategic internationalism of Rwandan heritage. *Journal of Eastern African Studies* 15 (3): 485–504.

Bolin, A. and D. Nkusi 2022. Rwandan solutions to Rwandan problems: Heritage decolonization and community engagement in Nyanza District, Rwanda. *Journal of Social Archaeology* 22 (1): 3–25.

Brandt, S. A. 2000. A tale of two world bank-financed dam projects in the horn of Africa. In *Dams and Cultural Heritage Management* (eds. S. A. Brandt and F. Hassan). Cape Town: World Commission on Dams, pp. 33–36.

Brockington, D. 2002. *Fortress Conservation: The Preservation of the Mkomazi Game Reserve, Tanzania*. Bloomington: Indiana University Press.

Brockington, D., R. Duffy, and J. Igoe 2008. *Nature Unbound: Conservation, Capitalism and the Future of Protected Areas*. London: Routledge.

Brown, W. 2015. *Undoing the Demos: Neoliberalism's Stealth Revolution*. London: Zed Books.

Brusius, M. and T. Rico 2023. Counter-archives as heritage justice: Photography, invisible labor and peopled ruins. *Journal of Visual Culture* 22 (1): 64–92. https://doi.org/10.1177/14704129221146494.

Brusius, M. and K. Singh 2017. Introduction. In *Museum Storage and Meaning: Tales from the Crypt* (eds. M. Brusius and K. Singh). Milton: Routledge, pp. 1–33.

Buller, A. 2022. *The Value of a Whale: On the Illusions of Green Capitalism*. Manchester: Manchester University Press.

Büscher, B. 2010. Derivative nature: Interrogating the value of conservation in 'boundless Southern Africa'. *Third World Quarterly* 31 (2): 259–276. https://doi.org/10.1080/01436591003711983.

Büscher, B., S. Sullivan, K. Neves, J. Igoe, and D. Brockington. 2012. Towards a synthesized critique of neoliberal biodiversity conservation. *Capitalism Nature Socialism* 23 (2): 4–30. https://doi.org/10.1080/10455752.2012.674149.

Campbell, I. 2009. *Physical Cultural Resources Safeguard Policy – Guidebook*. 1st ed. Washington, DC: World Bank.

Carruthers, W. 2022. *Flooded Pasts: UNESCO, Nubia, and the Recolonization of Archaeology*. Ithaca: Cornell University Press.

Cernea, M. M. 2001. *Cultural Heritage and Development: A Framework for Action in the Middle East and North Africa*. Washington, DC: World Bank.

Chalfin, B. 2001. Border zone trade and the economic boundaries of the state in north-east Ghana. *Africa* 71 (2): 202–224.

Chalfin, B. 2010. *Neoliberal Frontiers: An Ethnography of Sovereignty in West Africa*. Chicago: University of Chicago Press.

Childs, S. T. and D. M. Benden 2017. A checklist for sustainable management of archaeological collections. *Advances in Archaeological Practice* 5 (1): 12–25.

Chipangura, N. 2020. The politicization of liberation-struggle exhumations in eastern Zimbabwe: Spiritual evocation, patriotism, and professionalism. *Journal of Southern African Studies* 46 (5): 1037–1054.

Chipangura, N. and J. Mataga 2021. *Museums as Agents for Social Change: Collaborative Programmes at the Mutare Museum*. Milton: Taylor and Francis.

Chirikure, S., W. Ndoro, and J. Deacon 2018. Approaches and trends in African heritage management and conservation. In *Managing Heritage in Africa: Who Cares?* (eds. W. Ndoro, S. Chirikure, and J. Deacon). New York: Routledge.

Chiwaura, H. 2009. The development of formal legislation and the recognition of traditional customary law in Zimbabwe's heritage management. In *Legal Frameworks for the Protection of Immovable Cultural Heritage in Africa* (eds. W. Ndoro and G. Pwiti). Rome: ICCROM Conservation Studies 5, pp. 18–21.

Clack, T. and M. Brittain (eds.) 2018. *The River: Peoples and Histories of the Omo-Turkana Area*. Oxford: Archaeopress.

Clapham, C. 1996. *Africa and the International System: The Politics of State Survival*. Cambridge: Cambridge University Press.

Clapham, C. 2001. Rethinking African states. *African Security Review* 10 (3): 6–16.

Coffey, D. 2021. Māori are trying to save their language from Big Tech. *Wired*. www.wired.co.uk/article/maori-language-tech#:~:text=Well%20into%20the%2020th%20century,the%20same%20types%20of%20persecution, accessed 23 November 2023.

Collier, P. 2007. *The Bottom Billion: Why the Poorest Countries Are Failing and What Can be Done about It*. Oxford: Oxford University Press.

Collier, S. J. and A. Ong 2005. Global assemblages, anthropological problems. In *Global Assemblages: Technology, Politics, and Ethics as Anthropological Problems* (eds. A. Ong and S. J. Collier). Oxford: Blackwell, pp. 3–21.

Comaroff, J. and J. L. Comaroff 1991. *Of Revelation and Revolution, Volume 1: Christianity, Colonialism, and Consciousness in South Africa*. Chicago: University of Chicago Press.

Comaroff, J. L and J. Comaroff 2009. *Ethnicity, Inc*. Chicago: University of Chicago Press.

Coombe, R. J. 2013. Managing cultural heritage as neoliberal governmentality. In *Heritage Regimes and the State*, 2nd ed. (eds. R. F. Bendix, A. Eggert, and A. Peselman). Gottingen: Universitatsverlag Gottingen, pp. 375–388.

Coombe, R. J. and L. M. Weiss 2015. Neoliberalism, heritage regimes, and cultural rights. In *Global Heritage: A Reader* (ed. L. Meskell). Somerset: John Wiley & Sons, pp. 43–69.

Coombes, A. E. 2014. Monuments and memories: Public commemorative strategies in contemporary Kenya. In *Managing Heritage, Making Peace: History, Identity and Memory in Contemporary Kenya* (eds. A. E. Coombes, L. Hughes, and K. Munene). London: I. B. Tauris, pp. 139–183.

Cooper, F. 1997. Modernizing bureaucrats, backward Africans, and the development concept. In *International Development and the Social Sciences: Essays on the History and Politics of Knowledge* (eds. F. Cooper and R. Packard). Berkeley: University of California Press, pp. 64–92.

Cooper, F. 2002. *Africa since 1940: The Past of the Present.* Cambridge: Cambridge University Press.

Cooper, F. 2008. Possibility and constraint: African independence in historical perspective. *The Journal of African History* 49(2): 167–196.

Cooper, F. 2010. Writing the history of development. *Journal of Modern European History* 8 (1): 5–23.

Craig, D. and D. Porter 2006. *Development beyond Neoliberalism? Governance, Poverty Reduction and Political Economy.* Abingdon: Routledge.

Cross, C. and J. D. Giblin 2023. Introducing heritage for development: Practising the past in the pursuit of 'progress'. In *Critical Approaches to Heritage for Development* (eds. C. Cross and J. D. Giblin). Abingdon: Routledge, pp. 1–33.

Crossland, Z. 2014. *Ancestral Encounters in Highland Madagascar: Material Signs and Traces of the Dead.* Cambridge: Cambridge University Press.

Davies, M. I. J. and H. L. Moore 2016. Landscape, time and cultural resilience: A brief history of agriculture in Pokot and Marakwet, Kenya. *Journal of Eastern African Studies* 10 (1): 67–87.

De Cesari, C. 2020. Heritage beyond the nation-state? Nongovernmental organizations, changing cultural policies, and the discourse of heritage as development. *Current Anthropology* 61 (1): 30–56.

de Luna, K. 2016. *Collecting Food, Cultivating People: Subsistence and Society in Central Africa.* New Haven: Yale University Press.

De Sadeleer, N. 2021. Polluter pays principle. In *Essential Concepts of Global Environmental Governance* (eds. J.-F. Morin and A. Orsini). 2nd ed. Abingdon: Routledge, pp. 194–195.

Decker, C. and E. McMahon 2020. *The Idea of Development in Africa: A History.* Cambridge: Cambridge University Press.

Derbyshire, S. F. 2019. Trade, development and destitution: A material culture history of fishing on the western shore of Lake Turkana, Northern Kenya. *African Studies* 78 (3): 324–346.

Derbyshire, S. F. 2020. *Remembering Turkana: Material Histories and Contemporary Livelihoods in North-Western Kenya.* London: Routledge.

Dimier, V. 2014. *The Invention of a European Development Aid Bureaucracy: Recycling Empire.* Basingstoke: Palgrave Macmillan.

Dlamini, J. S. T. 2020. *Safari Nation: A Social History of the Kruger National Park.* Athens: Ohio University Press.

Duval, M. and B. Smith 2013. Rock art tourism in the uKhahlamba/Drakensberg World Heritage Site: Obstacles to the development of sustainable tourism.

Journal of Sustainable Tourism 21 (1): 134–153. https://doi.org/10.1080/09669582.2012.699060.

Ebron, P. A. 1999. Tourists as pilgrims: Commercial fashioning of transatlantic politics. *American Ethnologist* 26 (4): 910–932.

Ekeh, P. 2004. Individuals' basic security needs and the limits of democratization. In *Ethnicity and Democracy in Africa* (eds. B. Berman, D. Eyoh, and W. Kymlicka). Oxford: James Currey, pp. 22–37.

Elbourne, E. 2003. Words made flesh: Christianity, modernity, and cultural colonialism in the work of Jean and John Comaroff. *The American Historical Review* 108: 435–459.

Elias, O. and M. Wong 2021. Environmental impact assessment. In *Research Handbook on International Environmental Law* (eds. M. Fitzmaurice, M. Brus, and P. Merkouris). 2nd ed. United Kingdom: Edward Elgar, pp. 188–208.

Engmann, R. A. A. 2020. Coups, castles, and cultural heritage: Conversations with Flt Lieut. Jerry John Rawlings, former President of Ghana. *Heritage Tourism* 16 (6): 722–737.

Engmann, R. A. A. 2022. Contested heritage and absent objects: Archaeological representation at Ghana's forts and castles. In *The Oxford Handbook of Museum Archaeology* (ed. A. Stevenson). Oxford: Oxford University Press, pp. 197–220.

Erk, J. 2014. Federalism and decentralization in sub-Saharan Africa: Five patterns of evolution. *Regional & Federal Studies* 24 (5): 535–552. https://doi.org/10.1080/13597566.2014.971769.

Escobar, A. 2012. *Encountering Development: The Making and Unmaking of the Third World*. Princeton: Princeton University Press.

Ferguson, J. 1994. *The Anti-Politics Machine: 'Development', Depoliticization, and Bureaucratic Power in Lesotho*. Minneapolis: University of Minnesota Press.

Ferguson, J. 2006. *Global Shadows : Africa in the Neoliberal World Order*. Durham: Duke University Press.

Ferguson, J. 2010. The uses of neoliberalism. *Antipode* 41 (S1): 166–184.

Filippucci, P. 2009. Heritage and methodology: A view from social anthropology. In *Heritage Studies: Methods and Approaches* (eds. M. L. S. Sørensen and J. Carman). London: Routledge, pp. 319–325.

Folorunso, C. A. 2000. Third World development and the threat to resource conservation: The case of Africa. In *Cultural Resource Management in Contemporary Society: Perspectives on Managing and Presenting the Past* (eds. A. Hatton and F. P. MacManamon). 1st ed. London: Routledge, pp. 31–39.

Fontein, J. 2022. *The Politics of the Dead in Zimbabwe, 2000–2020: Bones, Rumours and Spirits*. Woodbridge: James Currey.

Foster, L. A. 2018. *Reinventing Hoodia Peoples, Plants, and Patents in South Africa*. Seattle: University of Washington Press.

Fredericks, R. 2018. *Garbage Citizenship: Vital Infrastructures of Labor in Dakar, Senegal*. Durham: Duke University Press.

Frey, M. and S. Kunkel 2011. Writing the history of development: A review of the recent literature. *Contemporary European History* 20 (2): 215–232.

Gabay, C. and S. Ilcan 2017. Leaving no-one behind? The politics of destination in the 2030 Sustainable Development Goals. *Globalizations* 14 (3): 337–342.

Gachuruzi, S. 2000. Large dams and the destruction of cultural heritage In Africa. In *Dams and Cultural Heritage Management* (eds. S. A. Brandt and F. Hassan). Cape Town: World Commission on Dams, pp. 25–26.

Gallagher, K. P. and F. Yuan 2017. Standardizing sustainable development: A comparison of development banks in the Americas. *Journal of Environment & Development* 26 (3): 243–271. https://doi.org/10.1177/1070496517720711.

Gavua, K. 2015. Monuments and negotiations of power in Ghana. In *The Politics of Heritage in Africa: Economies, Histories, and Infrastructures* (eds. K. Gavua, D. Peterson, and C. Rassool). New York: Cambridge University Press, pp. 97–112.

Gavua, K. and W. Apoh 2016. 'We will not relocate until our shrines and our ancestors come with us': Heritage and conflict management in the Bui Dam project area, Ghana. In *Community Archaeology and Heritage in Africa: Decolonizing Practice* (eds. P. Schmidt and I. Pikirayi). London: Routledge, pp. 204–223.

Giblin, J. 2017a. Performing 'indigenous' for international tourists who tour the rural poor. In *Archaeologies of 'Us' and 'Them': Debating History, Heritage and Indigeneity* (eds. C. Hillerdal, A. Karlström, and C.-G. Ojala). London: Routledge, pp. 241–257.

Giblin, J. 2017b. The performance of international diplomacy at Kigali Memorial Centre, Rwanda. *Journal of African Cultural Heritage Studies* 1 (1): 49–67.

Giblin, J. 2017c. Touring and obscuring poverty: Urban and rural cultural-heritage tourism. *Heritage & Society* 10 (2): 128–146. https://doi.org/10.1080/2159032X.2018.1495544.

Goldman, M. 2001. The birth of a discipline: Producing authoritative green knowledge, World Bank-style. *Ethnography* 2 (2): 191–217.

Goldman, M. 2005. *Imperial Nature: The World Bank and Struggles for Social Justice in the Age of Globalization*. New Haven: Yale University Press.

González, P. A. 2014. From a given to a construct: Heritage as a commons. *Cultural Studies* 28 (3): 359–390. https://doi.org/10.1080/09502386.2013.789067.

Gore, C. 2000. The rise and fall of the Washington Consensus as a paradigm for developing countries. *World Development* 28 (5): 789–804.

Habte, T. 2022. The Nigerian AI artist reimagining a stylish old age. *BBC News*. www.bbc.co.uk/news/world-africa-64260739, accessed 7 December 2023.

Hall, M. 1995. The legend of the lost city; or, the man with golden balls. *Journal of Southern African Studies* 21 (2): 179–199. https://doi.org/10.1080/03057079508708441.

Hall, M. and P. Bombardella 2005. Las Vegas in Africa. *Journal of Social Archaeology* 5 (1): 5–24. https://doi.org/10.1177/1469605305050141.

Hansen, T. B. and F. Stepputat 2001. Introduction: States of imagination. In *States of Imagination: Ethnographic Explorations of the Postcolonial State* (eds. T. B. Hansen and F. Stepputat). Durham: Duke University Press, pp. 1–38.

Harrison, G. 2004. *The World Bank and Africa: The Construction of Governance States*. London: Routledge.

Harrison, G. 2005. Economic faith, social project and a misreading of African society: The travails of neoliberalism in Africa. *Third World Quarterly* 26 (8): 1303–1320.

Harrison, G. 2019. Authoritarian neoliberalism and capitalist transformation in Africa: All pain, no gain. *Globalizations* 16 (3): 274–288.

Hart, G. 2001. Development critiques in the 1990s: *culs de sac* and promising paths. *Progress in Human Geography* 25 (4): 649–658.

Hart, G. 2002. *Disabling Globalization: Places of Power in Post-Apartheid South Africa*. Berkeley: University of California Press.

Harvey, D. 2002. The art of rent: Globalization, monopoly, and the commodification of culture. *Socialist Register* 38: 93–110.

Harvey, D. 2005. *A Brief History of Neoliberalism*. Oxford: Oxford University Press.

Hodge, J. M. 2007. *Triumph of the Expert: Agrarian Doctrines of Development and the Legacies of British Colonialism*. Athens: Ohio University Press.

Hodgson, D.L. 2011. *Being Maasai, Becoming Indigenous: Postcolonial Politics in a Neoliberal World*. Bloomington: Indiana University Press

Hountondji, P. J. 1995. Producing knowledge in Africa today: The Second Bashorun M. K. O. Abiola Distinguished Lecture. *African Studies Review* 38 (3): 1–10.

Huber, M. 2020. *Developing Heritage – Developing Countries : Ethiopian Nation-Building and the Origins of UNESCO World Heritage, 1960–1980*. München: De Gruyter.

Hughes, L. 2014. Sacred spaces, political places: The struggle for a sacred forest. In *Managing Heritage, Making Peace: History, Identity and Memory in Contemporary Kenya* (eds. A. E. Coombes, L. Hughes, and K. Munene). London: I.B. Tauris, pp. 99–138.

Hughes, L. 2018. Review of *The Politics of Heritage in Africa: Economies, histories, and infrastructures* ed. by Derek R. Peterson, Kodzo Gavua and Ciraj Rassool. *Africa* 88 (1): 183–184.

Humphris, J. and R. Bradshaw 2017. Understanding 'the community' before community archaeology: A case study from Sudan. *Journal of Community Archaeology & Heritage* 4 (3): 203–217. https://doi.org/10.1080/20518196.2017.1345364.

Hunter, E. 2016. Introduction. In *Citizenship, Belonging, and Political Community in Africa: Dialogues between Past and Present* (ed. E. Hunter). Athens: Ohio University Press, pp. 1–16.

Ibreck, R. 2013. International constructions of national memories: The aims and effects of foreign donors' support for genocide remembrance in Rwanda. *Journal of Intervention and Statebuilding* 7 (2): 149–169.

Ichumbaki, E. B. and E. Mjema 2018. The impact of small-scale development projects on archaeological heritage in Africa: The Tanzanian experience. *Conservation and Management of Archaeological Sites* 20 (1): 18–34. https://doi.org/10.1080/13505033.2018.133914.

Igoe, J. and D. Brockington. 2007. Neoliberal conservation: A brief Introduction. *Conservation and Society* 5 (4): 432–449.

James, D. 2014. *Money from Nothing: Indebtedness and Aspiration in South Africa*. Redwood City: Stanford University Press.

Jethro, D. 2020. *Heritage Formation and the Senses in Post-Apartheid South Africa*. London: Bloomsbury.

Jimenez, R. 2020. 'Slow revolution' in southern Africa: Household biosocial reproduction and regional entanglements in the history of cattle-keeping among Nguni-speakers, ninth to thirteenth century CE. *Journal of African History* 61 (2): 155–178.

Jopela, A. 2016. Conserving a World Heritage site in Mozambique: Entanglements between politics, poverty, development and governance on the Island of Mozambique. In *Urban Heritage and Sustainability: International Frameworks, National and Local Governance* (eds. S. Labadi and W. Logan). London: Routledge, pp. 37–56.

Jopela, A. 2017. The politics of liberation heritage in postcolonial southern Africa with special reference to Mozambique. Unpublished doctoral thesis, University of the Witwatersrand.

Josse-Durand, C. 2015. Le musée Konso au cœur de l'arène: Quand les court-iers en développement (re)dessinent les contours du champ politique éthiopien. *EchoGéo.* https://doi.org/10.4000/echogeo.14144.

Josse-Durand, C. 2018. The political role of 'cultural entrepreneurs' in Kenya: Claiming recognition through the memorialisation of Koitalel Samoei and Nandi heritage. *African Studies* 77 (2): 257–273. https://doi.org/10.1080/00020184.2018.1452859.

Josse-Durand, C. and A. Meckelburg 2022. Ruling over diversity: Federalism and devolution in Ethiopia and Kenya. In *Routledge Handbook of the Horn of Africa* (eds. J.-N. Bach, J. Abbink, and H. Mwakimako, et al.). Abingdon: Routledge, p. 255–268.

Joy, C. 2007. 'Enchanting town of mud': Djenné, a World Heritage Site in Mali. In *Reclaiming Heritage: Alternative Imaginaries of Memory in West Africa* (eds. F. de Jong and M. Rowlands). New York: Routledge, pp. 145–159.

Joy, C. 2010. Heritage and tourism: Contested discourses in Djenne, a World Heritage Site in Mali. In *Tourism, Power and Culture: Anthropological Insights* (eds. D. V. L. Macleod and J. G. Carrier). Bristol: Channel View Publications, pp. 47–63.

Joy, C. 2012. *The Politics of Heritage Management in Mali: From UNESCO to Djenné.* Walnut Creek: Left Coast Press.

Kabi, P. 2023. *Pollution, Profits, and the People.* Maseru: MNN Centre for Investigative Journalism.

Kamat, S. 2014. The new development architecture and the post-political in the Global South. In *The Post-Political and Its Discontents: Spaces of Depoliticisation, Spectres of Radical Politics* (eds. J. Wilson and E. Swyngedouw). Edinburgh: Edinburgh University Press, pp. 67–85.

Kamuhangire, E. 2005. Formal legislation and traditional management systems: A case of interdependence in Uganda. In *Legal Frameworks for the Protection of Immovable Cultural Heritage in Africa* (eds. W. Ndoro and G. Pwiti). Rome: ICCROM Conservation Studies 5, pp. 27–32.

Karega-Munene 2014. Origins and development of institutionalised heritage management in Kenya. In *Managing Heritage, Making Peace: History, Identity and Memory in Contemporary Kenya* (eds. A. E. Coombes, L. Hughes, and K. Munene). London: I.B. Tauris, pp. 17–51.

Karim, L. 2011. *Microfinance and Its Discontents: Women in Debt in Bangladesh.* Minneapolis: University of Minnesota Press.

Keitumetse, S. and O. Nthoi. 2009. Investigating the impact of World Heritage Site tourism on the intangible heritage of a community. *International Journal of Intangible Heritage* 4: 144–149.

Kenrick, J. and J. Lewis 2004. Indigenous peoples' rights and the politics of the term 'indigenous'. *Anthropology Today* 20 (2): 4–9.

Kersel, M. M. 2015. Storage wars: Solving the archaeological curation crisis? *Journal of Eastern Mediterranean Archaeology & Heritage Studies* 3 (1): 42–54.

King, R. 2019. How do African states think about cultural property? Revisiting management elites in southern Africa. *International Journal of Cultural Property* 26 (4): 387–411.

King, R. forthcoming. Loss revisionism and the disappearing past in Africa. In *Archaeology, Heritage, and the Decolonization of Africa's Past* (eds. A. B. Babalola and P. J. Lane). Athens: Ohio University Press.

King, R. and M. McGranaghan 2018. The archaeology and materiality of mission in southern Africa: Introduction. *Journal of Southern African Studies* 44 (4): 629–639.

King, R. and L. Nic Eoin 2014. Before the flood: Loss of place, mnemonics, and 'resources' ahead of the Metolong Dam, Lesotho. *Journal of Social Archaeology* 14 (2): 196–223.

Kiriama, H. 2021. Heritage management in East Africa. *Oxford Research Encyclopedia of Anthropology*. https://oxfordre.com/anthropology/display/ 10.1093/acrefore/9780190854584.001.0001/acrefore-9780190854584-e-286, accessed 6 November 2023.

Kiriama, H. 2023. Post-colonial archaeology in East Africa. In *Cultural Heritage Management in Africa: The Heritage of the Colonized* (eds. G. Abungu and W. Ndoro). Abingdon: Routledge, pp. 11–28.

Kiriama, H., I. Odiaua, and A. Sinamai 2010. Impact assessment and heritage management in Africa: An overview. In *Cultural Heritage Impact Assessment in Africa: An Overview* (eds. H. Kiriama, I. Odiaua, and A. Sinamai). Mombasa: Centre for Heritage Development in Africa, pp. 1–9.

Kirkwood, M. L. E. 2013. Postindependence architecture through North Korean modes. In *A Companion to Modern African Art* (eds. G. Salami and M. B. Visonà). London: Wiley, pp. 548–571.

Kirshenblatt-Gimblett, B. 2004. Intangible heritage as metacultural production. *Museum International* 56 (1–2): 52–65. https://doi.org/10.1111/j.1350-0775.2004.00458.x.

Kleinitz, C. and C. Näser 2011. The loss of innocence: Political and ethical dimensions of the Merowe Dam Archaeological Salvage Project at the Fourth Nile Cataract (Sudan). *Conservation and Management of Archaeological Sites* 13 (2–3): 253–280. https://doi.org/10.1179/175355211X13179154166231.

Kleinitz, C. and C. Näser (eds.) 2012. *'Nihna Nâs Al-Bahar – We Are The People of The River': Ethnographic Research in the Fourth Nile Cataract Region, Sudan*. Wiesbaden: Meroitica.

Labadi, S. 2011. Intangible heritage and sustainable development: Realistic outcome or wishful thinking? *Heritage & Society* 4 (1): 115–118.

Labadi, S. 2018. Historical, theoretical and international considerations on culture, heritage and (sustainable) development. In *World Heritage and Sustainable Development: New Directions in World Heritage Management* (eds. P. Larsen and W. Logan). London: Routledge, pp. 37–49.

Labadi, S. 2022. *Rethinking Heritage for Sustainable Development*. London: UCL Press.

Lafrenz Samuels, K. 2008. Value and significance in archaeology. *Archaeological Dialogues* 15 (1): 71–97. https://doi.org/10.1017/S1380203808002535.

Lafrenz Samuels, K. 2009. Trajectories of development: International heritage management of archaeology in the Middle East and North Africa. *Archaeologies* 5: 68–91.

Lafrenz Samuels, K. 2018. *Mobilizing Heritage: Anthropological Practice and Transnational Prospects*. Gainesville: University Press of Florida.

Landau, P. 1995. *The Realm of the Word: Language, Gender, and Christianity in a Southern African Kingdom*. Portsmouth: Heinemann.

Landau, P. 2000. Hegemony and history in Jean and John L. Comaroff's of Revelation and Revolution. *Africa* 70 (3): 501–519.

Landau, P. 2010. *Popular Politics in the History of South Africa, 1400–1948*. Cambridge: Cambridge University Press.

Lane, P. 2009. Environmental narratives and the history of soil erosion in Kondoa District, Tanzania: An archaeological perspective. *International Journal of African Historical Studies* 42 (3): 457–483.

Lane, P. J. 2015. Primordial conservationists, environmental sustainability, and the rhetoric of pastoralist cultural heritage in East Africa. In *Heritage Keywords: Rhetoric and Redescription in Cultural Heritage* (eds. K. Lafrenz Samuels and T. Rico). Boulder: University Press of Colorado, pp. 259–284.

Lane, P., C. Kleinitz, and Y. Gao 2016. Global frictions, archaeological heritage, and Chinese construction in Africa. In *The Routledge Handbook of Archaeology and Globalization* (ed. Tamar Hodos). 1st ed. London: Taylor and Francis, pp. 139–156.

Larkin, B. 2008. *Signal and Noise: Media, Infrastructure, and Urban Culture in Nigeria*. Durham: Duke University Press.

Larkin, B. 2013. The politics and poetics of infrastructure. *Annual Review of Anthropology* 42: 327–343.

Leach, M. and R. Mearns 1996. *The Lie of the Land: Challenging Received Wisdom on the African Environment*. Portsmouth: Heinemann.

Leloup, M. 2021. The culture bank in West Africa: Cultural heritage and sustainable development. In *African Heritage Challenges: Communities and Sustainable Development* (eds. B. Baillie and M. L. Stig Sørensen). London: Palgrave Macmillan, pp. 235–264.

Liuzza, C. and L. Meskell 2023. Power, persuasion and preservation: Exacting times in the World Heritage Committee. *Territory, Politics, Governance* 11 (7): 1265–1280.

Low, D. A. and J. M. Lonsdale 1976. Introduction: Towards a new order 1945–1963. In *History of East Africa, Volume 3* (eds. D. A. Low and A. Smith). Oxford: Clarendon Press, pp. 1–63.

Loxley, J. 2003. Imperialism and economic reform in Africa: What's new about the New Partnership for Africa's Development (NEPAD)?. *Review of African Political Economy* 30 (95): 119–128. https://doi.org/10.1080/03056240308373.

Luke, C. 2019. *A Pearl in Peril: Heritage and Diplomacy in Turkey.* New York: Oxford University Press.

Lunn-Rockliffe, S. 2020. Beyond the ruins of Embobut: Transforming landscapes and livelihoods in the Cherangani Hills, Kenya. *Journal of Contemporary Archaeology* 6(2): 274–296.

MacEachern, S. 2001. Cultural resource management and African archaeology. *Antiquity* 75 (290): 866–871.

MacEachern, S. 2010. Seeing like an oil company's CHM programme: Exxon and archaeology on the Chad Export Project. *Journal of Social Archaeology* 10 (3): 347–366.

Mahashe, T. G. 2019. MaBareBare, a rumour of a dream. Unpublished doctoral thesis, University of Cape Town.

Mamdani, M. 2018 [1988]. *Citizen and Subject: Contemporary Africa and the Legacy of Late Colonialism.* Princeton : Princeton University Press.

Manetsi, T. 2023. Heritage governance in post-colonial Africa. In *Cultural Heritage Management in Africa: The Heritage of the Colonized* (eds. G. Abungu and W. Ndoro). Abingdon: Routledge, pp. 57–69.

Masolo, D. A. 2010. *Self and Community in a Changing World.* Bloomington: Indiana University Press.

Mataga, J. 2019. Unsettled spirits, performance and aesthetics of power: The public life of liberation heritage in Zimbabwe. *International Journal of Heritage Studies* 25 (3): 277–297.

Mbembe, A. 2015. *On the Postcolony.* Johannesburg: Wits University Press.

Mbembe, A. 2016. Decolonizing the university: New directions. *Arts and Humanities in Higher Education* 15 (1): 29–45.

Meskell, L. 2009. The nature of culture in Kruger National Park. In *Cosmopolitan Archaeologies* (ed. L. Meskell). Durham: Duke University Press, pp. 89–112.

Meskell, L. 2012. *The Nature of Heritage: The New South Africa.* Malden: Wiley-Blackwell.

Meskell, L. 2014. States of conservation: Protection, politics, and pacting within UNESCO's World Heritage Committee. *Anthropological Quarterly* 87 (1): 217–243.

Meskell, L. 2018. *A Future in Ruins: UNESCO, World Heritage, and the Dream of Peace*. New York: Oxford University Press.

Meskell, L. 2021. Toilets first, temples second: Adopting heritage in neoliberal India. *International Journal of Heritage Studies* 27 (2): 151–169.

Meyer, B. 1999. *Translating the Devil: Religion and modernity among the Ewe in Ghana*. Edinburgh: Edinburgh University Press for the International African Institute.

Mkandawire, T. 2001. Thinking about developmental states in Africa. *Cambridge Journal of Economics* 25 (3): 289–314.

Mkandawire, T. 2015. Neopatrimonialism and the political economy of economic performance in Africa: Critical reflections. *World Politics* 67 (3): 563–612.

Mkandawire, T. and C. Soludo 2003. Introduction: Towards the Broadening of Development Policy Dialogue for Africa. *African Voices on Structural Adjustment*. Ottawa: Codesria International Development Research Centre, pp. 1–15.

Mokoena, N. 2017. Community involvement and heritage management in rural South Africa. *Journal of Community Archaeology & Heritage* 4 (3): 189–202. https://doi.org/10.1080/20518196.2017.1357233.

Monroe, J. C. and A. Ogundiran (eds.) 2012. *Power and Landscape in Atlantic West Africa: Archaeological Perspectives*. New York: Cambridge University Press.

Morris, D. 2014. Wildebeest Kuil Rock Art Centre, South Africa: Controversy and renown, successes, and shortcomings. *Public Archaeology* 13 (1–3): 187–199. https://doi.org/10.1179/1465518714Z.00000000068.

Mudimbe, V. Y. 1988. *The Invention of Africa: Gnosis, Philosophy, and the Order of Knowledge*. Bloomington: Indiana University Press.

Naffé, B. O. M., R. Lanfranchi, and N. Schlanger 2007. De Nouvelles perspectives pour l'archéologie preventive en Afrique: Introduction et remerciements. In *L'archéologie preventive en Afrique: Enjeux et Perspectives* (eds. B.O.M. Naffé, R. Lanfranchi, and N. Schlanger). Saint-Maur-des-Fossés: Éditions Sépia, pp. 15–19.

Ndlovu-Gatsheni, S. J. and W. Willems 2009. Making sense of cultural nationalism and the politics of commemoration under the Third Chimurenga in Zimbabwe. *Journal of Southern African Studies* 35 (4): 945–965.

Ndoro, W. 2001. Your monument, our shrine: The preservation of Great Zimbabwe. Unpublished PhD thesis, Uppsala University.

Ndoro, W. and H. Kiriama 2008. Management mechanisms in heritage legislation. In *Cultural Heritage and the Law: Protecting Immovable Heritage in English-Speaking Countries of Sub-Saharan Africa* (eds. W. Ndoro, A. Mumma, and G. Abungu). Rome: ICCROM, pp. 53–62.

Ndoro, W. and G. Wijesuriya 2015. Heritage management and conservation: From colonization to globalization. In *Global Heritage: A Reader* (ed. L. Meskell). Somerset: John Wiley & Sons, pp. 131–149.

Ndulu, B. J. 2008. The evolution of global development paradigms and their influence on African economic growth. In *The Political Economy of Economic Growth in Africa, Volume 1 1960–2000* (eds. B. J. Ndulu, S. A. O'Connell, R. H. Bates, P. Collier, and C. C. Soludo). Cambridge: Cambridge University Press, pp. 315–347.

Nhamo, A. and S. Katsamudanga 2022. Legal protection of African cultural heritage in the 21st century and beyond: A prognosis and futures perspective. In *Cultural Heritage Management in Africa: The Heritage of the Colonized* (eds. G. Abungu and W. Ndoro). Abingdon: Routledge, pp. 70–87.

Nic Eoin, L. and R. King 2013. How to develop intangible heritage: The case of Metolong Dam, Lesotho. *World Archaeology* 45 (4): 653–669. https://doi.org/10.1080/00438243.2013.823885.

Nixon, R. 2011. *Slow Violence and the Environmentalism of the Poor.* Cambridge, MA: Harvard University Press.

Odhiambo, E. 2002. The cultural dimensions of development in Africa. *African Studies Review* 45 (3): 1–16.

Ogot, B. A. 1999. *Building on the Indigenous: Selected Essays 1981–1998.* Kisumu: Anyange Press.

Ogundiran, A. 2014. The making of an internal frontier settlement: Archaeology and historical process in Osun Grove (Nigeria), seventeenth to eighteenth centuries. *African Archaeological Review* 31: 1–24.

Ojo, J., K. Ogueji, P. Stenetorp, D.I. Adelani 2023. How good are large language models on African languages? *arxiv*, https://doi.org/10.48550/arXiv.2311.07978.

Osei-Tutu, B. 2002. The African American factor in the commodification of Ghana's Slave Castles. *Transactions of the Historical Society of Ghana* 6: 115–133.

Payne, A. 2005 *The Global Politics of Unequal Development.* Basingstoke: Palgrave Macmillan.

Peterson, D. 2015. Introduction: Heritage management in colonial and contemporary Africa. In *The Politics of Heritage in Africa: Economies, Histories, and Infrastructures* (eds. K. Gavua, D. Peterson, and C. Rassool). New York: Cambridge University Press, pp. 1–36.

Piot, C. 2010. *Nostalgia for the Future: West Africa after the Cold War.* Chicago: University of Chicago Press.

Pitcher, A., Moran, M. H., and M. Johnston 2009. Rethinking patrimonialism and neopatrimonialism in Africa. *African Studies Review* 52 (1): 125–156.

Posnansky, M. 2000. The Volta Basin research project in Ghana 1963–70 and other West African dam projects: Learning from experience. In *Dams and Cultural Heritage Management* (eds. S. A. Brandt and F. Hassan). Cape Town: World Commission on Dams, pp. 36–37.

Radcliffe, S. 2006. Culture in development thinking: Geographies, actors, and paradigms. In *Culture and Development in a Globalising World: Geographies, Actors, and Paradigms* (ed. S. Radcliffe). New York: Routledge, pp. 1–29.

Ray, R. 2023. 'Small is beautiful': A new era in China's overseas development finance? GCI Policy Brief 017. Boston: Boston University Global Development Policy Center.

Ray, R. and R. Kamal 2019. Can south–south cooperation compete? The Development Bank of Latin America and the Islamic Development Bank. *Development and Change* 50: 191–220. https://doi.org/10.1111/dech.12468.

Rico, T. 2015. Heritage at risk: The authority and autonomy of a dominant preservation framework. In *Heritage Keywords: Rhetoric and Redescription in Cultural Heritage* (eds. K. Lafrenz Samuels and T. Rico). Boulder: University Press of Colorado, pp. 147–162.

Rico, T. and R. King forthcoming. 2024. Introduction: Epistemic journeys. In *Methods and Methodologies in Heritage Studies* (eds. R. King and T. Rico). London: UCL Press, pp. 1–13.

Rodney, W. 2012. *How Europe Underdeveloped Africa*. Oxford: Black Classic Press.

Rogerson, C. M. 1990. Sun International: The making of a South African tourism multinational. *GeoJournal* 22: 345–354.

Rose, N. 1999. *Powers of Freedom: Reframing Political Thought*. Cambridge: Cambridge University Press.

Roy, A. 2010. *Poverty Capital: Microfinance and the Making of Development*. New York: Routledge.

Saccaggi, B. and A. B. Esterhuysen 2014. Sekuruwe grave relocation: A lesson in process and practice. *South African Archaeological Bulletin* 69 (200): 173–181.

Salazar, N. B. and Y. Zhu 2015. Heritage and tourism. In *Global Heritage: A Reader* (ed. L. Meskell). Somerset: John Wiley & Sons, pp. 240–258.

Sanogo, K. 2007. Fondements et prémices d'une archéologie preventive au Mali. In *L'Archéologie Preventive en Afrique: Enjeux et Perspectives* (eds.

B. O. M. Naffé, R. Lanfranchi, and N. Schlanger). Saint-Maur-des-Fossés: Éditions Sépia, pp. 97–99.

Saugestad, S. 2001. *The Inconvenient Indigenous: Remote Area Development in Botswana, Donor Assistance and the First People of the Kalahari*. Uppsala: Nordic Africa Institute.

Schmidt, E. 2018. *Foreign Intervention in Africa after the Cold War: Sovereignty, Responsibility, and the War on Terror*. Athens: Ohio University Press.

Schmidt, P. R. 2017. *Community-Based Heritage in Africa: Unveiling Local Research and Development Initiatives*. New York: Routledge.

Schoenbrun, D. 2021. *The Names of the Python: Belonging in East Africa, 900 to 1930*. Madison: University of Wisconsin Press.

Schramm, K. 2010. *African Homecoming: Pan-African Ideology and Contested Heritage*. Walnut Creek: Left Coast Press.

Schwartz, P. 2015. Principle 16. In *The Rio Declaration on Environment and Development: A Commentary* (ed. J. E. Viñuales). 1st ed. Oxford University Press, pp. 429–450.

Skosana, D. 2019. Grave matters: The contentious politics of gravesite removals in contemporary South Africa – the case of Tweefontein, Ogies. Unpublished PhD thesis, University of the Witwatersrand.

Smith, L. 2013. *Making Citizens in Africa: Ethnicity, Gender, and National Identity in Ethiopia*. New York: Cambridge University Press.

Snowball, J. D. and S. Courtney 2010. Cultural heritage routes in South Africa: Effective tools for heritage conservation and local economic development? *Development Southern Africa* 27 (4): 563–576. https://doi.org/10.1080/0376835X.2010.508589.

Stiglitz, J. E. 1988. Economic organization, information, and development. In *Handbook of Development Economics, Volume 1* (eds. H. Chenery and T. N. Srinivasan). Amsterdam: North-Holland, pp. 93–160.

Taylor, E. C. 2021. Risk and labour in the archives: Archival futures from Uganda. *Africa* 91 (4): 532–552.

Thamae, M. L. and L. Pottinger (eds.) 2006. *On the Wrong Side of Development: Lessons Learned from the Lesotho Highlands Water Project*. Morija: Transformation Resource Centre.

Thrift, N. 2006. Re-inventing invention: New tendencies in capitalist commodification. *Economy and Society* 35 (2): 279–306.

Tischler, J. 2013. *Light and Power for a Multiracial Nation: The Kariba Dam Scheme in the Central African Federation*. New York: Palgrave Macmillan.

United Nations Economic Commission for Africa (UNECA) 2005. Review of the application of environmental impact assessment in selected African countries. Addis Ababa: UN.ECA. https://hdl.handle.net/10855/5607, accessed 17 November 2023.

van Waarden, C. 1996. The pre-development archaeology programme of Zimbabwe. In *Aspects of African Archaeology: Papers from the 10th Congress of the PanAfrican Association for Prehistory and Related Studies* (eds. G. Pwiti and R. Soper). Harare: University of Zimbabwe, pp. 829–836.

Vidal, F. and N. Dias 2016. Introduction: The endangerment sensibility. In *Endangerment, Biodiversity and Culture* (eds. F. Vidal and N. Dias). London: Routledge.

Waterton, E. and L. Smith 2010. The recognition and misrecognition of community heritage. *International Journal of Heritage Studies* 16 (1–2): 4–15. https://doi.org/10.1080/13527250903441671.

Watts, M. 2006. Culture, development, and global neo-liberalism. In *Culture and Development in a Globalising World: Geographies, Actors, and Paradigms* (ed. S. Radcliffe). New York: Routledge, pp. 30–57.

Weiss, L. M. 2014. The historical narration of rights in South Africa: Past, present, and future tense. *Heritage & Society* 7 (2): 121–138.

Wiegratz, J. 2016. *Neoliberal Moral Economy: Capitalism, Socio-Cultural Change, and Fraud in Uganda*. Lanham: Rowman & Littlefield.

Wiegratz, J., G. Martiniello, and E. Greco 2018. Introduction: Interpreting change in neoliberal Uganda. In *Uganda: The Dynamics of Neoliberal Transformation* (eds. J. Wiegratz, G. Martiniello, and E. Greco). London: Zed Books, pp. 16–40.

Wiegratz, J., J. Mujere, and J. Fontein 2022. The case for oral histories of neoliberal Africa. *Third World Thematics: A TWQ Journal* 7 (4–6): 199–221.

Williamson, J. 1993. Democracy and the 'Washington consensus'. *World Development* 21 (8): 1329–1336.

Wingfield, C. 2018. Articles of dress, domestic utensils, arms and other curiosities: Excavating early 19th-century collections from southern Africa at the London Missionary Society Museum. *Journal of Southern African Studies* 44 (4): 723–742.

Winter, T. 2013. Clarifying the critical in critical heritage studies. *International Journal of Heritage Studies* 19 (6): 532–545.

Witz, L. 2006. Transforming museums on postapartheid tourist routes. In *Museum Frictions: Public Cultures/Global Transformations* (eds. I. Karp, C. A. Kratz and L. Szwaja, et al.). Durham: Duke University Press, pp. 107–134.

Yang, H., B. A. Simmons, R. Ray *et al.* 2021. Risks to global biodiversity and indigenous lands from China's overseas development finance. *Nature Ecology and Evolution* 5: 1520–1529. https://doi.org/10.1038/s41559-021-01541-w.

Young, C. 1994. *African Colonial States in Comparative Perspective*. New Haven: Yale University Press.

Zetterström-Sharp, J. 2020. Imagining future agricultural landscapes in a new Sudan: Entitled expertise, cultural intransience and fine warm rain in the English wilds. *History and Anthropology* 31 (3): 293–313.

Zetterström-Sharp, J. and P. Basu 2015. Complicating culture for development: Negotiating 'dysfunctional heritage' in Sierra Leone. In *Museums, Heritage and International Development* (eds. P. Basu and W. Modest). London: Routledge, pp. 56–82.

Acknowledgements

This Element was written as part of projects funded by the Leverhulme Trust (RPG-2021–180) and the Arts and Humanities Research Council of the United Kingdom (AH/W001381/1). I am grateful to the series editors and to reviewers for their constructive feedback.

Cambridge Elements ☰

Critical Heritage Studies

Kristian Kristiansen
University of Gothenburg

Michael Rowlands
UCL

About the Series

This series focuses on the recently established field of Critical Heritage Studies. Interdisciplinary in character, it brings together contributions from experts working in a range of fields, including cultural management, anthropology, archaeology, politics, and law. The series will include volumes that demonstrate the impact of contemporary theoretical discourses on heritage found throughout the world, raisingawareness of the acute relevance of critically analysing and understanding the way heritage is used today to form new futures.

Cambridge Elements ≡

Critical Heritage Studies

Elements in the Series

Printed in the United States
by Baker & Taylor Publisher Services